THE FIRST
JOB HUNT
SURVIVAL GUIDE

THE FIRST JOB HUNT SURVIVAL GUIDE

Winning Advice on Choosing and Getting the Job You Want

EDITED BY

Pat Morton and Marcia R. Fox, Ph.D.

A DIVISION OF DRAKE BEAM MORIN, INC.
New York

Contents

foreword

Many people manage their careers as if they were blind-folded and throwing darts at a career choice "dart board." Are you the type of person who will say, "Wherever it lands will be my destiny"? That is not how it needs to be done.

The management of your career is one of the most important activities in which you will ever participate. Whether it is securing your first position following college graduation or exploring a new career direction, you have taken the important first step.

Of course, after several months of networking, sending out more resumes than you care to think about, getting some of the inevitable rejection letters, having some interviews, and one or two nibbles from prospective employers, this may not appear to be all that great an adventure after all.

Has it occurred to you that your job search may actually be more difficult than the work you will be doing after somebody hires you to work in his or her organization? It could well be true. The important thing to realize is that for now, your job is to find and secure a career position—not just a job. The truth is that it will likely take you longer than it did your counterparts, or even you, a decade ago. Such is the state of the career market in the 1990s.

The July 12, 1993 issue of *Fortune* magazine reported on the economy and job prospects for graduating seniors, saying both have been bleak for four years running. All the numbers are down; total job offers, offers per graduate, recruiter visits per campus, number of campuses visited, and starting salaries. As we move into the latter part of the 1990s and enter the first years of the twenty-first century, we realize that things will probably not change very much. But despite the gloom and doom, the future is still full of opportunity for those willing to put some effort into their careers.

The *Fortune* article added, "Recession and restructuring have done more than cut the jobs available to seniors. They have permanently changed the way graduates and employers seek each other out. Students unaware of these changes—or unwilling to play by a new set of rules—are striking out cold."

This book was written to give you an edge in locating employment in a tight and changing job market, and to give you the skills in career management that will be vital to you, not just now but throughout your working life. Keep it and refer to it as you progress through your career journey. Think of it as a compass to guide you and show you the way down your new career path.

This is a just a beginning. You can make it a good one. Good luck!

PART I

CHOOSING THE JOB

CHAPTER 1

Personal Assessment

*"Cheshire Puss," (she) began, "would you please tell me
which way I ought to go from here?"
"That depends on where you want to get to," said the Cat.
"I don't much care where . . . ," said Alice.
"Then it doesn't matter which way you go," said the Cat.*

—LEWIS CARROLL,
Alice in Wonderland

These words reinforce the need to have a plan for managing your career. Without it, you may end up in a place much different from where you want to be. Another question that is often asked, sometimes in jest and sometimes in seriousness, is, "What do you want to be when you grow up?" It is often asked of kids as they develop through their teens, and it comes up among adults who have already spent years in the workplace. The inference is that the person being asked the question has not really found his or her way as an employed adult. And while you may not always feel like it, you *are* grown up—at least in the eyes of our society. You now have a college degree and, most likely, a large student loan debt to go along with it. You

3

now find yourself with not only the economic pressures to get a job but pressure from family, friends, and peers to get on with your life. The career search begins.

Career management may seem to be a relatively easy process. But it is not. There are three main questions that you will need to answer as you begin this journey:

1. Where am I now?
2. Where do I want to be?
3. How will I get there?

Because you will spend the next forty to fifty years of your life working, the work you do needs to be more than a job. In the words of that famous anthropologist, Margaret Mead, "A job is something you get paid to do. A vocation is something you would pay somebody to let you do if you weren't getting paid to do it." Why not concentrate your time and efforts on looking for a vocation rather than just a job? We all know people who struggle in jobs they truly dislike, but fear quitting because they need the income, want the security, or are afraid of change. How sad! And how essential for you to avoid such a situation.

You can avoid such a prospect by choosing your career directions carefully—assessing your abilities, your interests, experience, and even your passions in life—and then matching all that with the career possibilities that exist today. Your educational background is important, but it need not be an absolute in determining your livelihood. Many career options are open to the educated person who is eager to learn and grow in a position. This is especially true for liberal arts graduates and those with degrees in the social sciences. The exact subject matter you have studied may be less important than the study habits, skills, and experience you gained either in the classroom and laboratory or while working during and after your college years.

There are many college students and people already in the work force who have given little thought to their careers. When asked what kind of job they'd like, their responses often include: "I don't know what I want to do but I want to make a lot of money," or "Just tell me where the jobs are and I can sort it out." The current state of the job market in many areas probably has a lot to do with their inability to plan or make good career decisions. They are frightened by the difficulties encountered. For many people, the real problem is not knowing where to begin. If you feel that either description typifies your feelings and fears (or even comes close), there are options to help you with the task.

> *"The most important thing about goals is having one."*
> —Geoffrey F. Abert

In many cases, recent college graduates who have had little luck in finding a job think about going to graduate school. According to Kevin Harrington, director of the Career Services Office of the Harvard Graduate School of Education, "I have spoken with many students who think graduate school is the answer to their problems. In fact, all too often they don't have a career direction that brings them to graduate school. Recent graduates need to identify for themselves the reasons for going to graduate school. What I have found is that in many cases, the student comes out of graduate school being overqualified educationally and underqualified in terms of experience. Many employers now look at this candidate in terms of qualifying for more senior positions, which, of course, they don't because of the limited experience." Mr. Harrington adds, "My recommendation to anyone thinking of graduate school is to get at least two years of work experience first. It will increase the value and level of understanding of that graduate educational experience."

According to *Job Choices: 1995*, published by the National Association of Colleges and Employers (62 Highland Avenue, Bethlehem, PA 18017, 800–544–5272), in an article entitled "Identifying Your Strengths," "You can't put together an effective resume or perform well in an interview if you can't identify and discuss your strengths. Where do you find your strengths? Examine the skills you've acquired and use with proficiency."

Begin writing down some answers to the questions below. As you work through these questions, others are likely to come to mind. Jot down answers to those as well.

What have I accomplished during school, in part-time and full-time jobs, in volunteer, community, or social activities, that will be meaningful to a prospective employer? Write specific descriptions of as many as you can now and add to the list later as you recall others.

What skills did those accomplishments demonstrate that will add value to a prospective employer? As you extract skills from your accomplishments, you'll find some occurring over and over. These are your primary skills—the ones that make up your unique skill profile.

What is unique about me that will make me stand out from the crowd? Think about situations where you were singled out because of your special qualities in some arena. Define your "unique selling proposition."

In order to be truly happy in whatever chosen career direction you take, you need to have some passion for it. The happiest, most successful people have a passion for what they do. They look forward to going to work, to performing their jobs. You need to identify where your passion is and what gets you excited. Are you willing to take the risk to find a career that gets the fire inside you burning? Are you willing to do what it takes—education, training, experience, etc.—to make it happen? Only you can answer these questions.

Another question that needs to be answered is how much money you need to live. This is very different than how much money you want to make. The career position that may provide passion and a sense of satisfaction may not provide as much money. You need to come to grips with that reality and be willing to accept the trade-off, if necessary. Not everyone is willing to do it. Are you?

"In order to succeed, we must first believe that we can."
—MICHAEL KORDA

In addition, there are numerous excellent resources that can help you identify your strengths, interests, and abilities. However, please note that many of the instruments listed below, while not available to the individual, may be accessed through a college career office, an educational or testing psychologist, or another career professional. Also, it is important to realize that the results of many of these same inventory instruments should be interpreted only by a trained, even a certified, professional.

The Myers-Briggs Type Indicator® is a self-administered multiple-choice survey that identifies your personality type—whether you are introverted or extroverted, fact-based or intuitive, analytical or emotional. This instrument can help you better understand your special strengths, and the type of work you might enjoy and be successful in doing.

The World of Work Inventory (WOWI) is a comprehensive, multi-dimensional, career assessment instrument developed to aid people in better understanding themselves in relation to the total world of work. The inventory, which was derived from the Department of Labor's database, consists of three distinct yet integrated scales: Career Interest Activities, Job Satisfaction Indicators, and Vocational Training Potentials. Based on each individual's unique responses, suitable job recommendations are selected from the 12,000+ possible occupations listed in the *Dictionary of Occupational Titles*—the ultimate source of job descriptions in the United States. The materials are available from World of Work, Inc., 64 East Broadway Road, Suite 175, Tempe, AZ 85252. As with many of the assessment tools discussed, a professional counselor should help interpret the results.

The Campbell Interest and Skill Survey is a measure of self-reported interests and skills. Its major purpose is to help individuals understand how their interests and skills map into the occupational world, thereby helping them make better career choices.

John L. Holland's Self-directed Search (SDS) is a comprehensive vocational interest inventory that may help lead you to a career choice or confirm an occupational preference. The Occupations Finder, a part of SDS, lists 1,346 occupations, including all of the most common occupations in the United States in the late 1980s. A companion *Dictionary of Occupational Titles* (*DOT*), which can be found in most libraries, employment and college career centers, presents descriptions of occupations and estimates of interests, aptitudes, and educational requirements associated with each one.

Discover is a computer-based program available at many college and university career centers and at public libraries that have career divisions. Discover contains extensive information on some 450 different occupations. By interacting with this computer program, you can move through a step-by-step exercise in career decision-making—gaining valuable knowledge about your interests, values, and abilities.

The Occupational Outlook Handbook, updated biennially by the Bureau of Labor Statistics of the U.S. Department of Labor, lists more than 200 occupations and such descriptions as the nature of the work, working conditions, present employment, training requirements, job outlook, and typical earnings for each.

As was stated earlier, you should be very careful about doing these formal assessments strictly on your own. It is too easy to misinterpret results, get confused by the data, or end up feeling more lost and confused than when you started. Many people find that options become much clearer when they meet with a professional career counselor. Most colleges and universities have career centers and placement offices with trained professionals who can be of assistance, usually at no cost or at a reasonable fee for students and alumni. Job counseling services can also be found through the Yellow Pages in your telephone company's directory. If you use a job counseling service, be sure to identify the fees and get references before agreeing to become a client. If you prefer, you can contact the National Board of Certified Counselors for a listing of certified career counselors in your area (3D Terrace Way, Greensboro, NC 27403, 910–547–0607).

After you've been tested, examined, checked, and certified . . . after you've run the computer programs and read the literature . . . you still have some questions to answer and some decisions to make: "Where does the rest of my life begin? What am I going to do now that I am no longer a student?"

WHAT DOES IT ALL MEAN?

By now, you're probably wondering what the results of all the assessment tests and personal soul-searching mean in terms of getting a job!

Organizations seeking to hire for a position go to great lengths to define the skills and qualities needed to succeed in that position. They examine job responsibilities, stakeholders in the results of the work, personal characteristics needed for success in the team or work group—all for the purpose of developing a comprehensive profile of what the successful candidate will look like.

The purpose of your assessment work is very similar—to help you develop a comprehensive profile of what the right job for you will look like. If this sounds a bit strange to you—"I need a job; I can't be picky about whether it's the right one for me or not!"—think about how much happier and productive you'll be in the *right* job—the one that's good for both you and the employer.

"The people who get on in this world are the people who get up and look for the circumstances they want, and, if they can't find them, make them."
—GEORGE BERNARD SHAW

Use what you've learned about yourself through the formal assessment instruments and your self-analysis to develop a "picture" of what your ideal job would look like. Incorporate such tangibles as location, size and type of organization, job responsibilities, reporting structure, compensation, amount of travel, match of job with your skill set, etc. Also include intangibles that are important to you—things like organizational culture, work style, type of boss and co-workers, etc.

Describe your ideal job profile in writing. It will give you a starting point around which to structure your job search and also give you a benchmark against which to measure opportunities.

It's *Your* Decision

There are many options available to you. Everyone has multiple talents and abilities and areas that are of interest.

There are many job opportunities available that will make use of those abilities. For some, because there are so many choices, the answers are sought through other people and other means. The experienced relative who seems to have all the answers, people who are actually working in the desired field, the multitude of psychological testing instruments, and yes, even astrological horoscopes. We often defer to these rather than trust our own knowledge and understanding. But you know better than anyone else what is appropriate for you. The self-assessment process gives you guidance and suggestions, but it needs to feel right.

Whatever direction you choose to take, it is important that you control it. These are major decisions that directly impact you and also the people around you—specifically, your family. But remember, if you are happy, satisfied, and feel good about your decisions, your family will also benefit. No one knows better than you what is best for you. That doesn't mean that you should ignore the collective wisdom of others, but measure it with your own.

There is a story of a man who was offered a job many years ago for which he was well qualified. The job was going to pay a lot of money for that time but was located on the other side of the country. He turned down the job because family members, specifically his wife, said it was not a good decision to move so far away from home. For many years after, the man questioned whether he made the right decision. He would often ask, "Would life have been different had I taken that job?" There is no way of knowing the answer to that question, but had he made the decision himself, he may well have taken the position and not looked back wondering "What would have happened if . . . ?"

Setting Goals

Once you have your ideal job profile, it's time to set some goals about how to attain it. Start with the general career goal statements below:

1. What I want to be doing one year from today is:

_____

_____

_____

2. What I want to be doing five years from today is:

_____

_____

_____

3. What I want to be doing ten years from today is:

_____

_____

_____

When setting goals, the following guidelines should help.

- Be as specific and concrete as possible about what you want to do.
- Set a target date or time to reach your goals. Set intermediate dates for large goals and projects. In addition, you need to set start dates for beginning

the process, many people forget to do this and the end result is not as successful as desired.

- Choose goals that are attainable and realistic. You want them to be challenging but not out of reach.

- Reward yourself for achieving your goals. Reward others who contribute to your reaching your goals and solutions.

Big Firm or Small Company?

Once you've decided what to do, the next logical question is often, "Where to do it?" We're not referring to geography here—you probably already have a good idea in which part of the country you want to work. This refers to the size of the organization you want to join. There are relative merits to companies of every size—the large corporate entity, the mid-size firm, and even the small shop of fewer than fifty people—in many cases, a lot fewer than fifty.

It's a good idea to recall the recent past: mergers, acquisitions, and the attendant downsizing that has inevitably followed ownership changes among large companies make them far less stable employers than they once were. Huge layoffs are announced with alarming regularity. And corporate debt has ballooned—all making job security within many of the *Fortune 500* companies a dim memory.

The fastest growing segment of the job marketplace is in the smaller company. According to John Kniering, director of the Career Center at the University of Hartford, "Eighty percent of jobs that college students get upon graduation are with employers who have fewer than one hundred employees."

The cover story of the November 1994 issue of *Inc.* was entitled, "What Business Would You Start Today?" Over sixty leading experts in the field were asked that question. A few common themes emerged from the answers. Many people will be involved in telecommuting, working from home and commuting to the office via fax and modem. There will be jobs in areas where the needs of the consumer are rapidly changing. And the line between work and home will become more blurred. "The merger between work and life will offer opportunities to companies that can help people—or their own employees—manage the blur."

"Use what talents you possess; the woods would be very silent if no birds sang there except those that sang best."
—HENRY VAN DYKE

Over the last ten years, the *small* companies—those with fewer than five hundred employees—were responsible for adding the most new jobs to the economy. Larger organizations also added positions but at the same time deleted an equal number and in many cases more positions than were added. How many people do you know who are still working for larger organizations? According to Anthony P. Carnevale, executive director of the Institute for Workplace Learning in Alexandria, Virginia, five out of every six American workers now earn paychecks from companies with fewer than a thousand employees (*America and the New Economy*, Jossey-Bass, 1991).

Many agree this is where the immediate future lies—

with the smaller firm. In an article in *National Business Employment Weekly*, Special College Career Edition, Fall 1992, Karen B. Andrews, career services director at Kennesaw State College in Marietta, Georgia, concurred, "The opportunities are with new, small, up-and-coming companies." Of course, available positions in these firms will be fewer per company, but the competition for those positions may also be lighter than that within larger firms.

Few small or middle-size companies—and almost assuredly no small-size firms—have the personnel or resources to recruit on campus. So unless someone in your family or close circle of friends owns or works in one, you may have little information about the benefits—and the possible drawbacks—of working for a smaller company.

Students sometimes have the image of the small firm as a mom-and-pop operation in which members of the family run everything and new hires are overworked and underpaid. However, many of the available business publications over the past few years have reported that this impression is unfounded and that the dangers of being overworked and underpaid may actually be more applicable to large companies.

Many who *do* work for smaller firms indicate that they have the opportunity to perform a wide variety of tasks and assume greater responsibilities early in their careers. The very nature of small companies rewards the generalist rather than the specialist. This gives new employees the opportunity to gain valuable hands-on experience, mastering a diversity of skills early on. This can be a boon to their careers.

Interestingly, entry-level positions within smaller organizations often pay surprisingly well—often at least on a par with similar positions in much larger companies.

True, the benefits may be fewer, and there may be less perceived job security than with a very large firm; however, one must ask just how much job security is there today in a firm of *any* size?

Also, though these firms may not offer much in the way of training programs, it is also true that larger companies, which once had extensive, formal training for entry-level personnel, have been cutting back these programs in recent years, placing new employees in more productive positions much earlier.

One of the benefits of working for the smaller employer is the opportunity to develop close, personal, and caring relationships with one's fellow workers—even with the managers and owners of the company. Recent college graduates who miss the collegiality of the campus may find the close-knit environment within the small company much more comfortable than the comparatively sterile, much more formal atmosphere of a firm employing thousands.

Though few small companies recruit on campus, as noted earlier, many do rely on college placement offices for resume referrals and the posting of job listings. Networking, however, is likely the most productive avenue for locating a position with a smaller employer.

Conducting a national job search among smaller companies is still possible. The following reference books provide an excellent resource:
• *The Hidden Job Market*, 4th ed. (1995, Peterson's) lists 2,000 fast-growing high-tech companies.
• *Ward's Business Directory of U.S. Private and Public Companies* (1992, Gale Research) is a guide to

> 133,000 companies—90 percent of which are privately owned.
> • *America's Fastest Growing Employers*, 2nd. ed (1994, Adams) profiles 700 high-growth organizations.
> • *Technology Resource Guide—1994 Edition* (Corporate Technology Information Services) lists 35,000 high-tech companies, including 22,000 that employ fewer than one thousand people each.

There is one more thing that you need to do before you venture too far into the job-hunting jungle. Get yourself a reasonably decent telephone answering machine. Some key things to consider: day/time stamp—to let you know when the person called; toll saver feature—so you can find out if you have messages from a distance without incurring a charge; and maximum length of incoming message—some machines cut the caller off after thirty seconds. Make sure that the outgoing message is appropriate. It may be something like, "You have reached [phone number] and no one is available to answer the phone. Please leave your name, phone number, and a brief message at the sound of the beep. Thank you." Make sure you check your messages at least once a day. And return phone calls to prospective employers promptly.

CHAPTER 2

Working in the '90s and Beyond:

The Changing Nature of Work and the Workplace

CAREER PROSPECTS TODAY: WHAT'S HOT AND WHAT'S NOT

Most career counselors and consultants agree that today's college graduates entering the work force will change careers three to five times during their working lives. This does not mean just changing jobs but changing the focus of their careers. For example, an individual may start out as an accountant, then become a business owner (in a field other than accounting), and then become a teacher. In addition, most people today will change employers between seven and ten times during their working lifetimes.

The implications of this information are important: the truth is that you are unlikely to make the long-term, lifetime commitment to a profession or an employer that your parents and grandparents made. The *job for life* concept no longer works. Although it's how you now need to focus on employment in one field or another, this career decision isn't one you will have to live with for the rest of your life.

Moreover, experts say that many of today's graduates entering the labor force could well end their careers working in a discipline that may not even exist today. Consider such recent developments as genetic engineering, virtual reality, and multi-media computer applications. As recently as the early 1980s these would have been considered the stuff of science fiction. Yet today these new disciplines are earning high profits and are poised for exponential growth. In fact, many career experts predict that nearly half of the workforce will have jobs in ten years that do not exist today.

In today's career landscape no one can say with any degree of certainty what he or she will be doing in twenty years. Change is happening more rapidly than in any time in our history, and new jobs will surface to manage and respond to those changes.

For now, however, your primary objective is to find a position in a career that will take full advantage of your education, experience, self-assessment, and interests. For most people, that means selecting a job in a field that exists *today* but has the latitude and opportunity for you to develop the skills and gain the experience for the positions that will be in demand *tomorrow*.

So Where Are the Jobs?

The growth in jobs is in the service sector. According to an article in the *Wall Street Journal* on Monday, February 27, 1995, the fastest growing professions are human services workers, computer engineers, computer systems analysts, physical therapists, and paralegals. The article went on to list thirty-five other professions that will experience fast growth through the year 2005. The vast majority of these positions were service-related. The top forty are all highly paid or very highly paid professions with low to very low jobless rates.

In an article published in the April 11, 1995, issue of *USA Today*, many of the best jobs to have in the future are tied to the computer and technology world. The job that heads the list is multimedia software design; these "jobs have grown 40 percent in ten years and there's still only 30,000 out there."

Along these lines, *Tomorrow's Jobs*, a pamphlet reprinted from the Labor Department's *Occupational Outlook Handbook* (printed annually), suggests that "service-producing industries, including transportation, communications, and utilities; retail and wholesale trade; services; government; and finance, insurance, and real estate, are expected to account for approximately 23 million of the 24.6 million new jobs created between 1990 and the year 2005." To put that number in perspective, a total of 33 million jobs were created during the fifteen years from 1975 to 1990.

"In addition," the publication notes, "the services division within this sector, which includes health, business and educational services, contains sixteen of the twenty fastest growing industries, and twelve of the twenty industries adding the most jobs. Expansion of service sector employment is linked to . . . changes in consumer tastes and preferences, legal and regulatory changes, advances in science and technology, and changes in the way businesses are organized and managed."

Employment within the services division is expected to

grow by nearly 35 percent by 2005, accounting for almost one-half of all new jobs. The two largest industry groups in this division—health services (nursing and other specialties) and business services—are projected to continue very rapid growth. Computer programming and other computer technology–related jobs are also expected to grow. Social, legal, engineering, and management services industries illustrate the service division's strong growth for the future.

In addition, the article "The 1992-2005 Job Outlook in Brief," published by the Bureau of Labor Statistics in the *Occupational Outlook Quarterly/Spring 1994*, indicated the following for three categories of opportunity:

Demand Expected to Exceed Supply

Adult education teachers

Chiropractors

Computer scientists and systems analysts

Construction and building inspectors

Cost estimators

Counselors

Engineering, science, and data processing managers

Funeral directors

Health services managers

Human services workers

Inspectors and compliance officers (except construction)

Loan officers and counselors

Metallurgical, ceramic, and materials engineers

Occupational therapists

Pharmacists

Physical therapists

Physician assistants

Podiatrists

Property and real estate managers

Recreational therapists

Registered nurses

Respiratory therapists

Restaurant and food service managers

Roman Catholic priests

Schoolteachers—secondary and special education

Speech and language pathologists and audiologists

Veterinarians

Demand Expected to About Equal Supply

Accountants and auditors

Agricultural scientists

Chemical engineers

Chemists

Civil engineers

College and university faculty

Dietitians and nutritionists

Economists and marketing research analysts

Electrical and electronics engineers

Employment interviewers

Geologists and geophysicists

Hotel managers and assistants

Industrial engineers

Industrial production managers

Landscape architects

Mechanical engineers

Meteorologists

Mining engineers

Nuclear engineers

Optometrists

Petroleum engineers

Rabbis

Retail managers

Schoolteachers—kindergarten and elementary

Social scientists and urban planners

Social workers

Sociologists

Underwriters

Urban and regional planners

Writers and editors

Supply Expected to Exceed Demand

Actuaries

Administrative service managers

Aerospace engineers

Architects

Archivists and curators

Biological and medical scientists

Budget analysts

Dentists

Designers

Education administrators

Financial managers

Foresters and conservation scientists

Lawyers and judges

Librarians

Management analysts and consultants

Marketing, advertising, and public relations managers

Mathematicians

Personnel, training, and labor relations specialists and managers

Photographers and camera operators

Protestant ministers

Psychologists

Public relations specialists

Purchasers and buyers

Radio and television announcers and newscasters

Recreation workers

Reporters and correspondents

Statisticians

Surveyors

Visual artists

The Department of Labor offers the following forecasts for other service-oriented industries during the period from 1992 through the year 2005:

Retail trade employment up by 26 percent; wholesale trade to increase by 16 percent.

Finance, insurance, and real estate employment— increasing by 21 percent.

Employment in transportation, communications, and public utilities—up by 15 percent.

Government employment—excluding public

education and public hospitals—is expected to increase 14 percent.

Among goods-producing industries, overall employment is not expected to show any appreciable change, though growth prospects within this sector vary considerably.

The construction industries are expected to be the only goods-producing industry in which employment will increase. The gain through 2005 is projected to be 18 percent.

Manufacturing employment is expected to decline by three percent from the 1990s level of 19.1 million workers. Further, the composition of manufacturing employment is expected to shift, in that most of the disappearing jobs will be in production. However, the number of professional, technical, and managerial positions in manufacturing companies will increase.

Overall employment in agriculture, forestry, fishing, and mining has been declining for years and is expected to continue to decline by about six percent through 2005.

Key Point

In summary, the growth prospects are in the service sector, especially health care and business services, where nearly half the new jobs will be created. Manufacturing and goods-producing industries, with the exception of the construction industries, will experience little if any growth and may even decline in many areas.

However, most of the jobs that become available over the next decade or so won't be created by an increase in the size of the total workforce. The Labor Department forecasts that most jobs will be born of replacement needs. This means that even occupations with little or no employment growth—or slower than average employment growth—may still offer many job openings. Replacement openings occur as people leave their occupations, some to transfer to other occupations as a step up the career ladder or to change careers. Others stop working in order to return to school, assume household responsibilities, or to retire. Even full-employment will find at least two to three percent of the population in some transition mode between jobs and employment opportunities.

"The greatest thing in this world is not so much where we are, but in what directions we are moving."
—OLIVER WENDELL HOLMES

Occupations with high replacement openings are generally within large employment groups where pay, status, and training requirements are all low, and where the proportion of young and part-time workers is high. Occupations with relatively few replacement openings tend to be those with high pay, status, and training requirements. These same low replacement occupations tend to have high proportions of prime working age, full-time workers. Among professional specialty occupations, for example, only 46 percent of total job opportunities will result from replacement needs.

This suggests that well-educated, highly paid people tend to hold on to their jobs longer. Your aspirations lead you to pursue these types of positions, and because the numbers of these well-educated job holders have been increased by the baby boomers, you will be competing for fewer job openings than generations past. As a result, a successful job search will require you to invest more energy, have greater flexibility, and develop a more focused strategy. The end results will be worth the investment.

Recruiting Trends 1994-1995, written by Patrick Scheetz, Director of the Collegiate Employment Research Institute of Michigan State University, is a report on data collected from 545 business, industry, and government organizations that employ new college graduates. According to this report, "The growing occupations and employment categories in the current job market for new college graduates are computer related occupations, engineering, sales and marketing, accounting and finance, and medical and health care services." The top ten occupational fields include:

Computers— these occupations will focus on local area networks, management information systems, personal computer programming, and undetermined (as yet) occupations that will focus on the information superhighway.

Engineering— all of these occupational areas will be in demand for the next few years.

Accounting and Finance— the market is good for entry-level positions as financial analysts, claims representatives, accountants, and other fields such as change management and human resources management.

Sales and Marketing— the occupations in this field will be for both inside sales such as retail and outside sales that include buyers and representatives.

Medical and Health Services— there will be a significant need for nurses, physician assistants, physical therapists, rehabilitation specialists, occupational therapists, and many more.

Environmental— waste and environmental management will continue to be major areas of concern that will increase the number of career opportunities. Some of these will include waste disposal systems specialists, hazardous waste transportation, and environmental health and safety.

Sciences and Mathematics— these occupations will include chemistry, chemical processing, and actuarial positions.

Economic and Community Development— there will be a need for people skilled in areas such as community planning, transportation, and legal administration.

Communication and Telecommunication— there will be numerous opportunities in this field, including wireless data, satellite, switching systems, and digital signal processing.

Hotel, Restaurant, and Leisure— people will have more free time, and this industry will continue to grow.

John Kniering, director of the Career Center at the University of Hartford, says, "The shelf life of a job title is much shorter today than it was even ten years ago." He goes on to say that today's job hunter needs to "think about what people do and where they do it rather than what it is called."

"The hot jobs will focus on client server environments, services for the aging baby-boom generation, and social needs," he indicates. According to Mr. Kniering, the jobs within those areas include interactive television, networking, systems, and internet interfacing on the technology end; health services and technology and long-term care for the aging population; and new roles, as yet to be defined, to satisfy the needs of the population. There will also be jobs available to address "the crises that have befallen our schools and educational institutions."

"Many high school and college graduates lack many of the skills needed to compete today, never mind tomorrow," he adds. "Educational programs and educators will be in demand, as will assessment specialists to diagnose and assess special needs and to develop new tests and evaluation tools."

"Too many people are thinking of security instead of opportunity. They seem more afraid of life than death."
—JAMES F. BYRNES

The traditional manufacturing jobs will diminish except in the technology fields such as robotics, computer aided design and manufacturing (CAD/CAM), and quality improvements. Automation and off-shore production will be more profitable for many manufacturers. The small job shops will still operate, but they will usually employ only a small handful of people.

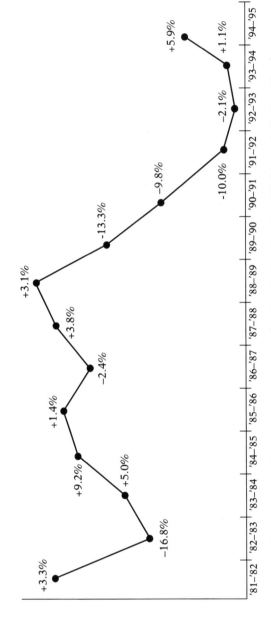

HIRING INTENTIONS AMONG EMPLOYERS
OF NEW COLLEGE GRADUATES

+3.3%
−16.8%
+9.2%
+5.0%
+1.4%
−2.4%
+3.8%
+3.1%
−13.3%
−9.8%
−10.0%
−2.1%
+1.1%
+5.9%

'81–'82 '82–'83 '83–'84 '84–'85 '85–'86 '86–'87 '87–'88 '88–'89 '89–'90 '90–'91 '91–'92 '92–'93 '93–'94 '94–'95

SOURCE: Scheetz, L. Patrick. 1994. *Recruiting Trends 1994-95.* East Lansing, Michigan: Collegiate Employment Research Institute. Michigan State University.

In many organizations, centralized information processing operations are becoming a thing of the past. They are being replaced by networked PCs that are staffed by people with specific business expertise. Satellite links will enable an organization to communicate with its offices around the world.

What Employers Are Looking For

The trend for new college graduates, according to Dr. Scheetz and *Recruiting Trends 1994-1995*, tends to be somewhat optimistic, with an anticipated "slight improvement in hiring intentions. During the previous four years, demand for new college graduates had declined."

The following chart indicates which academic majors will likely face a favorable, competitive, or very competitive supply and demand ratio as they enter the job market.

ESTIMATED JOB DEMAND BY FIELD OF STUDY
1994–95
BACHELOR'S DEGREE GRADUATES

Academic Majors	Estimated Numbers	Percent of Total
FAVORABLE SUPPLY/DEMAND RATIO		
Business and Management	266,280	22.8%
Engineering	65,656	5.6%
Health Professions	63,138	5.4%
Computer and Information Sciences	26,721	2.3%
Engineering Technologies	18,357	1.6%
Physical Sciences	17,411	1.5%
Total Graduates	**457,562**	**39.2%**

Academic Majors	Estimated Numbers	Percent of Total
COMPETITIVE SUPPLY/DEMAND RATIO		
Education	118,258	10.1%
Mathematics	15,618	1.3%
Protective Services	17,903	1.5%
Architecture and Environmental Design	10,420	0.9%
Communications Technologies	1,224	0.1%
Other	16,541	1.4%
Total Graduates	**179,964**	**15.4%**
VERY COMPETITIVE SUPPLY/DEMAND RATIO		
Social Sciences	133,047	11.4%
Communications	55,022	4.7%
Psychology	62,267	5.3%
Letters	56,333	4.8%
Life Sciences	42,111	3.6%
Visual and Performing Arts	44,587	3.8%
Liberal/General Studies	28,435	2.4%
Multi/Interdisciplinary Studies	23,067	2.0%
Home Economics	16,484	1.4%
Public Affairs	18,084	1.6%
Agriculture and Natural Resources	13,981	1.2%
Foreign Languages	12,885	1.1%
Philosophy and Religion	7,793	0.7%
Theology	5,127	0.4%
Parks and Recreation	4,327	0.4%
Area and Ethnic Studies	4,925	0.4%
Total Graduates	**528,474**	**45.3%**
GRAND TOTAL—All Fields	**1,116,000**	

SOURCE: Scheetz, L. Patrick. *Recruiting Trends 1994–95.* East Lansing, Michigan: Collegiate Employment Research Institute, Michigan State University.

According to the June 1995 issue of *Inc.* magazine, in a survey conducted by the University of Pennsylvania and the National Center on the Educational Quality of the Workforce, "Attitude and communication skills ranked well above test scores when 3,000 employers were asked what they considered in hiring nonsupervisory and production workers." On the five-point scale used (with five being very important), both of these averaged over four, with previous work experience a close third. The areas with scores of three or less included years of schooling completed, scores on tests administered as part of the interview, academic performance (grades), experience or reputation of the applicant's school, and teacher recommendations.

"Do not follow where the path may lead. Go instead where there is no path and leave a trail."

—ANONYMOUS

Demise of the Paternalistic Employer

The days are long gone when you worked for a company from graduation to retirement. In very rare instances this may hold true, but for the vast majority, a resume will list at least four or five employers over a working career. In some cases it could be far more. Even in Japan, the bastion of "employment for life," there are far fewer employees staying with a company their entire careers. In fact, most people today do not expect to stay with one employer. The challenges and growth opportunities desired by many are not always available. In addition, employers often can't maintain the workforce levels of days gone by due to economic conditions, automation, changes in technology, changes in customer demand for products and services, and a multitude of other reasons. The employers cannot guarantee that you will have a job forever either.

As was stated earlier, many of the jobs of tomorrow have yet to be invented. The only thing for certain is that change *will* happen. Those individuals who are flexible, willing and able to learn new skills, and willing to use and enhance their existing skills in new ways will reap the rewards of the future.

To believe that job security can truly exist is not a realistic position. Certainly there are some organizations that have hired smart and rarely let people go for reasons other than performance. But those organizations are exceptions. This is not intended to paint a bleak picture, only a realistic one. During the early 90s, every time you picked up a newspaper, you'd find an article or two about this company *downsizing*, that company going through a *reengineering*, or another company *restructuring*. All those euphemistic terms probably mean the same thing; jobs are being eliminated and people are being displaced. But there is a silver lining to the dark cloud if you are willing to put the effort into managing your career.

The changing workplace of the '90s also has serious implications for the way you conduct your job search. The fact that so many people have lost their jobs permanently in the 1980s and '90s also means that there are many fewer traditional jobs out there in general. As a result, access has become much more difficult. You'll need to rethink your strategy for your job search and consider some of the new opportunities for getting a foot into an organization or field. These include wearing quasi-entrepreneurial hats such as:

1. Working as a temporary at a desired company, either by direct solicitation to the company or by working for a temp agency. (Call the personnel department of companies that interest you and find out what agencies they use.)

2. Seeking assignments as an independent contractor on a "project" basis. This is a good strategy if you have a contact within a company who can find out about opportunities or get you work or if you have "ready to go" skills for hire that you are willing to package more entrepreneurially.

Because employers are often skittish about making hiring mistakes, a surprising number increasingly pick many full-time employees from their temporary labor force. You can also use this temp strategy to your advantage: you both get to know each other to see if there's a good fit.

Another dramatic change in the workplace that will affect you in your job search is the inconsistent and varied technologies employers are likely to use. Some will still have secretaries; many will block your access with voice mail, and still others will use a combination of voice mail and a live person, such as staff at a reception or message desk. Whatever the situation, you'll need to polish your telephone message skills into a smooth, succinct, appealing delivery.

Equally important, you'll have to be *endlessly and politely persistent* if you don't get called back. Chances are your potential contacts consider you low on their priority list. Frequently they are retrieving their messages while on the road or in a high-pressure deadline situation. Many workers who used to be polite with everyone are no longer able to get their jobs done in today's leaner organization and still remember to call everyone back. Don't expect good manners and you won't be disappointed. Just plan to push forward and persevere until you get through. But stay cheerful and polite—it's crucial.

What More Can You Do?

With competition for entry-level positions becoming greater every year, many are finding that sometimes "little things mean a lot." Having two applicants for the same position—recent graduates with virtually identical academic scores and backgrounds—may encourage savvy employers to look beyond courses and obvious qualifications to help them decide whom to hire. For example:

Internships. This says that you know something about the world of work, but more importantly, it says you know something about their business if you have interned with a firm in the field. It also says that you are committed to working in this field and you are serious about your career. Companies are looking to hire people with proven experience. The cost of replacing a bad hire can be astronomical, so companies are becoming more selective in their hiring practices. According to Ed Ryan, president of Marketing Personnel Research, Inc., "it can cost a company up to three times the employee's annual salary if the person hired turns out to be the wrong person."

The internships assist companies with this process. In the larger organizations (*Fortune 500*), for example, as many as 50 percent of those hired right out of school served in an internship capacity either at the hiring company or at another company in the industry. If you are reading this book and are still in school and you haven't served an internship yet, it may not be too late. You could use the summer before graduation, or a semester that is part of your senior year. It doesn't have to be a full-time activity and you don't have to receive monetary compensation. The experience alone will be worth it.

Volunteerism. Most colleges and universities have a variety of volunteer activities available to students. The surrounding communities are always looking for bright, energetic people to help with a multitude of projects. At the University of Hartford, for example, there is a program called Education Main Street. Students volunteer two to four hours per week to tutor middle school and high school students in a variety of subjects. Most campuses have blood drives, food bank activities, and other functions that not only broaden your experience but enable you to take on leadership roles, solve problems, and work in a team environment, all of which are desired by most employers. You can still volunteer some of your time.

"Experience is a hard teacher, because she gives you the test first, the lessons afterwards."
—VERNON LAW

Clubs and organizations. Do you or did you belong to any club or organization on campus? Did you serve in any type of leadership capacity? The skills developed while a member of many campus organizations can be directly transferred to the work environment. Think about what you did and how you did it. Many of the clubs and organizations are student chapters of professional affiliations, such as the American Marketing Association, the American Society for Training and Development, and others. Not only can you develop worthwhile skills and gain experience, you can also learn about the profession that you are about to enter.

Published papers. Whether in scholarly journals or even in industry trade papers, publication credit sets you apart from everyone else. Again, it may not be too late to get in print. And researching and writing something for the field you hope to join may prove to be a very worthwhile complement to your summer job search.

Neatness counts. Your professors may never have been sticklers for the visual appearance or style of your papers and other academic work, but don't count on that being the case in the race for a quality position that pays well. Check every cover letter and resume for details. Correct spelling and punctuation, the agreement of subjects and predicates, and an appealing overall visual impression of yourself on paper all go a long way to saying, "This is a person who is serious about doing the job right the first time."

Present yourself professionally in person, too. Of course, you're going to wear your "earnest" suit to interviews. But again, look at the details. The cleanliness and grooming of your hair and nails make an important first impression on employers and their representatives. Your shoes should be recently shined. These may seem like minor details to you, but to those on the other side of the desk it indicates something about your self-discipline and feelings of self-worth. Two other areas of importance are a firm handshake (not a bone crusher) and good eye contact (but don't stare). Both of these indicate confidence and strong feelings of self-acceptance. Of course, a nice suit, good grooming, a firm handshake, and good eye contact won't get you a job. But your failure to observe some of these basics could easily eliminate you from further interviews and the opportunity to present your skills.

Watch what you say. Remember that interviews don't end when the interviewer puts the pen down and closes the notebook. Those unguarded moments are often the most telling ones of all about a job candidate. There is nothing "off the record" in these situations. So if you don't want it to be remembered and perhaps "played back" later on, don't say it. Interviewers aren't your friends—not yet, anyway. And the focus of much of their job is the disqualification of candidates; don't give them that chance with a thoughtless or mean-spirited comment.

There is an old saying, "What you are speaks so loudly, I can't hear what you're saying." In today's employment climate, perhaps more than at any time in the recent past, it's important to project a professional image all the time you're "on" in front of a potential employer. Interviewers often make judgments of an applicant's suitability based on the first minute or two of observation and interaction. Once you've passed this "initial inspection," what you say becomes increasingly important. If you fail that initial inspection, what you say will be discounted or ignored. In fact, you will have been eliminated; the rest of the interview, no matter how polite, will be nothing more than a formality.

CHAPTER 3

Your Career Planning and Placement Office

ITS ROLE AND RESPONSIBILITIES

The role of the college career center or placement office has been changing rather dramatically in recent years. It used to be the place where you would go to get career testing and perhaps help with a resume. According to John H. Kniering, director of the Career Center of the University of Hartford, "We act as a centralized unit of the university to help all students with a wide range of career, educational, and job concerns." He continues, "Career planning at the college level is a multifaceted process in and of itself, touching upon such concerns as choosing an appropriate major, selecting a part-time job, exploring cooperative education or internship placements, and assessing one's values, interests, and skills, and then relating them to career options."

The campus career center becomes a focal point for many members of the greater academic community. Students drop in to get guidance; faculty and staff stop by to learn more about what interests students and to learn more about the trends in the job market; and employers and business people lend their knowledge and expertise as well as conduct on-campus interviews.

Mr. Kniering indicates that one of the areas he strongly encourages students to get involved with is the informational interview. (For more information on this topic, turn to page 135.) "Because many students at the university are from other states, we have developed an extensive list of alumni in the area who are more than willing to meet with current students for information interviews. Students can look through a loose-leaf binder to find the names of people in most professions who are very willing to help."

"Success comes in cans. Failure comes in can'ts."

—FRED SEELY

Networking continues to be the most efficient and effective method of finding a job. Most campus career centers strongly encourage their students to develop their networks. Two ready-made components are their fellow students and the members of the faculty. In addition, a connection with graduates and alumni further expands an individual's network.

The National Association of Colleges and Employers—the association serving collegiate career centers—conducts a quadrennial survey of its 1,518 member offices nationwide. Those responding to the most recent audit (823, or 54.2 percent) provided the following overview of services offered by such organizations nationally.

SERVICES OFFERED THROUGH CAREER PLANNING AND PLACEMENT CENTERS

	Percent of Respondents
Career Counseling	94.2
Occupational and employer information library	93.7
Placement of graduates into full-time employment	93.4
Campus interviewing	91.6
Placement of students into summer and part-time jobs	83.2
Placement of alumni	82.7
Credential service	71.9
Resume referral	71.6
Cooperative education, intern, experiential program	62.8
Resume booklets	56.3
Vocational testing	52.1
Computerized candidate data base	48.2
Career planning or employment readiness course for credit	31.6
Academic counseling	28.7
Dropout prevention and counseling	16.2

In addition, many career centers also offer career information fairs, conduct workshops (on a variety of career development and job search topics), and have on-line services that connect students through the Internet with employment opportunities all over the country and even the world.

RECRUITING ACTIVITIES

	Percent of Respondents
Allow employers to pre-screen candidates	71.6
Sponsor career days	68.0
Sponsor job fairs	61.0
Work directly with third-party recruiters	44.8
Inform employers of their services through mass mailings, phone calls, personalized letters and visits	38.6
Fewer companies recruiting on campus vs. previous year	54.3

Regarding the data, various individuals indicated that the numbers for 1995 are about the same or slightly lower in some areas, especially campus recruiting visits.

About a third of the respondents charge students specific fees for services, and 36 percent charge alumni such fees. More than one-fifth (22 percent) charge employers for specific services (up from 9 percent in 1987)—primarily for participation in career days and fairs.

Nearly two out of three graduating students have used the career centers on campus to help them with their career concerns. In fact, more than one out of three students obtain jobs through the centers and one out of five is offered a job as a result of on-campus recruiting activities. The latter number is declining due to the declining numbers of on-campus recruiting visits.

Mr. Kniering indicates, "There are fewer campus visits by recruiters from various companies because there are fewer corporate recruiters. In recessionary times, the first jobs to be eliminated in most organizations are the college recruiting and training positions. This has an impact on what we can offer the students in terms of on-campus interviews." He goes on to say, "There seems to be a more targeted focus. For example, a few years ago we would have seventy-five to one hundred campus visits, but the following year we had half that many."

The greatest problems reported by the placement center offices were budget and staff constraints. Clearly, the majority of such offices are doing their best to do a great deal with insufficient resources.

New Ways of Assisting Students and Employers

Most campus career centers offer students more than the traditional "job hunting help when you are ready to graduate." Dick Hess, director of the Career Development and Placement Center at Susquehanna University, has created a guide. "I created and use this document in presentations for both parents and students who plan to enter college as new, first year students. It stems from research conducted over the past ten years regarding what employers consistently say are their major hiring criteria. It is basic and to the point and the response, especially from parents, has been wonderful." The handout that Mr. Hess provides is entitled *Gaining the Competitive Edge: Six Strategies for Succeeding in Your Career Choice*. Inside, he briefly talks about six keys to success:

- Study a foreign language
- Develop project management skills
- Enhance your oral and written communication skills
- Gain a working knowledge of computers and computer software
- Develop a strong sensitivity to both diversity and the global marketplace
- Secure a minimum of one career-related work experience while in college.

At most schools, during the orientation session for incoming first year students, representatives from the career center discuss the services offered and what students can learn by stopping by. Two major areas typically covered are student employment and cooperative education/ internship programs.

"The secret of getting ahead is getting started."
—ANONYMOUS

The Student Employment Office helps students find part-time and summer jobs so they can better meet their educational expenses. The staff members of these offices actively seek employment opportunities from the community and post them so that students can easily see what is available. Students then have the option to apply for the position directly or seek assistance from the career center. In addition, most campuses have college work-study and campus employment programs that provide students with additional income opportunities.

The Cooperative Education/Internship program may differ slightly from campus to campus. Basically it is an educational program that integrates academic study with related professional training and experience. In some cooperative education programs, students will work for a semester and then attend classes for a semester. In other programs, the student will work part-time (10–20 hours a week) while pursuing full-time academic study. The length of the co-op (as it is often called) program is usually up to the student. In some cases it will last one semester, one year, or a couple of years. Most institutions require third-year status to qualify for the program. Many of the co-op programs are coordinated through the department of the students' major, and the experience is supervised by a faculty member or advisor so the students will not only be monetarily compensated but also receive appropriate academic credit for their work. Not all co-op experiences earn credit. You need to check with your career center and academic department.

In many cases, the co-op process continues until the students graduate. Often, the students in the co-op program are hired into full-time positions by their respective employers. The primary objective of the program is to provide an appropriate classroom education while allowing students to explore possibilities, make informed career decisions, and prepare for entry into the job market.

The Internship Program is related to the Cooperative Education Program but differs in a few ways. Most internships are for one semester or academic term (although some can extend for an academic year), are usually unpaid, and require faculty involvement because the students are working for credit as well as experience. It is important that the internship creates a meaningful experience for the student. While making photocopies may be a critical component of a job, it would not be an appropriate role for an internship if that was all the student did.

Many employers benefit from getting involved with cooperative education and internship programs because they have bright, energetic students working on projects that often have been sitting on the back burner because no one has had the time to work on them, regardless of how valuable the project could be to the company. Kevin Harrington, director of the Career Services Office at the Harvard Graduate School of Edcuation, wholeheartedly concurs. "Internships and the practicum are excellent ways for the student and the employer to mutually benefit from the experience. Students learn and apply their knowledge to real-life situations. These are great items to list on the resume."

"To succeed do the best you can, where you are, with what you have."
—THEODORE ROOSEVELT

Many campuses have student chapters of national organizations. In other cases, professional organizations charge students a discounted fee for belonging to the organization directly. For example, many campuses have student chapters of the American Marketing Association. They have meetings, bring in speakers, and work with the local chapters and national association to give students a real-world experience.

Many colleges and universities have implemented a Mentoring Program. Business leaders from the area get involved with incoming first-year students and establish a mentoring relationship with them. The intent is for the students to meet with their mentors at least once a semester to discuss issues and concerns and for the mentors to share insights and experiences. This program gives the students a greater understanding of the world of business and gives the business professionals a sense of satisfaction from being able to help students through their college years.

Clearly, the role of the college career planning and placement center has changed substantially in the past couple of decades, and that role is still evolving. The emphasis today is more and more on information exchange—using every means possible to inform students, alumni, faculty, and employers of each other's needs, capabilities, and offerings. Innovation and computerization have changed the way both the career office and its clients work.

However, one thing is still as true today as it ever was: your college career center can only assist you in finding a position. It can't get a job for you. You are still the only one who can do that.

According to Dr. Phillip J. Decker, associate professor at the University of Houston–Clearlake, "the best advice that I could give to students is to work hard. Put the effort into your studies while in school and into your job search activities after you graduate. And then, when you get that job, work hard to learn everything that you can about the industry and the organization. Give your employer 110 percent. Too many people don't take their careers seriously."

PART II

GETTING THE JOB

CHAPTER 4

Your Resume

According to an article entitled "Read Between the Lines" in the June 1995 issue of *Inc.* magazine, "No one wants to waste time interviewing job candidates who won't pan out. Four chief executives of growing companies shared with us some of the more inventive screens they apply to resumes." These four executives include Steve Rosenbaum, president of a news network, who looks for candidates with spirit and energy; Kathy Ericksen, president of an electronics distributor, who firsts interviews candidates over the phone and always asks the same eight "extremely characterological" questions to see how prospective employees will respond; David Blumenthal, president of an information technology company, who wants people who want to be the best and who build relationships quickly; and finally Gary Hirshberg, president of a yogurt manufacturer, who looks for self-starters.

These are just a few examples of what works today and will work tomorrow in the job hunt. You need to differentiate yourself from the field of job seekers. You want the people doing the hiring to take notice of what you have to offer. The first place to start is with a quality resume.

This is an essential document in the job search. The resume is a combination of pedigree, dossier, press release, and promotional device. It is your advertisement, your marketing tool. Do not underestimate the importance of a good, effective resume. It will not get you a job—only you can do that. But a good resume and an effective cover letter may sufficiently interest a potential employer (or, most likely, a recruiter or applicant "screener" for that employer) to invite you to interview for a position. Remember, few if any people are ever hired without an interview.

Most recruiters are overwhelmed with resumes and job inquiries. As a result, your resume, especially if it is unsolicited, will get a quick review. You need to be aware that one of the primary responsibilities of those people who screen resumes is to find reasons to eliminate job seekers from further consideration. Of course, they won't admit this publicly. Typically, the initial resume review will last no more than fifteen to thirty seconds. If you are lucky, your resume may be reviewed for a longer period of time, but don't count on it.

A decision is then made about your viability and your resume ends up in one of three piles: yes, no, or maybe. Your first responsibility in constructing your resume is simple—don't give them any reasons to put you in the no pile (which, by the way, is almost always the largest of the three stacks). At the very least, you want to be in the maybe pile. This pile is then re-sorted into either a yes or a no.

For those jobs that require good written communication skills, your resume and the cover letter that accompanies it can be great showcases of your writing talents. When you send your resume to a prospective employer, it *is* you—on paper. As such, it is just as important in creating a good first impression as over-the-phone or face-to-face contacts. If you have succeeded in gaining an interview without sending your resume ahead of you—perhaps through the personal recommendation of a network contact—your resume is a good leave-behind piece to remind the employer of you after the interview.

"If you want to double your success rate, just double your failure rate."
—TOM WATSON

The resume is a distilled and organized compilation of your education, selected experiences and achievements, and your skills and abilities. Properly ordered, these elements should translate what you have done in the past to what you can do in the future for an employer. Reading it, the employer (or his or her representative) should easily be able to discern:

- Who you are
- The type of work you seek
- What you know
- What you have learned and done
- What you are capable of doing

A successful resume will project something of your own spirit and uniqueness. It will also speak to the needs and interests of the employer—focusing on skills and abilities that are important to the needs and experiences relevant to the available position.

The first thing resume readers usually notice is the overall appearance of the document. If it's sloppy, overly crowded, or full of errors, there's an excellent chance they won't even read it. Such a document presents you in a very negative light. To help you make this determination, put your resume on the wall and step back about ten feet. It may sound silly, but ask yourself this question: "Does my resume look good?" Does it look neat from a distance, or does it seem crowded and messy? If you can honestly answer yes, that is terrific. If the answer is no, then you need to do some work. Here's a quick checklist to help ensure that you make a good first impression on paper.

Your Resume Should Be:

Neat and clean, with at least one-inch margins on top, bottom, and sides. Don't be afraid of "white" space. Don't overdo the white space, either.

Easy to read. The print size should never be smaller than 10–point type for eye comfort. Bold-faced and underlined items can enhance readability, but they should never be overdone. Don't bold-face and underline the same item.

Flawless, with no spelling errors or typos. Read it, reread it, and read it once more to be sure. Most word-processing programs have a spelling-check program built in; use it.

No more than two pages. A single page is preferred for entry-level job candidates.

Written on a word processor if at all possible.
The appearance is much more professional than
can be achieved using a typewriter. This also makes
changes and updates easier to accomplish. If you
don't have a word processing system, many libraries
have one available. You need to supply your own
diskettes on which to store the information.

**Printed on high quality bond or laser printer
paper.** Make sure your color choices are limited to
white, off-white, ivory, or very light gray. Do not use
pastel papers or any bright colors. Make sure you
print it on a laser printer whenever possible, and on
the same quality and color paper as your cover
letter.

Your own work. Don't let anyone else write your
resume. You know yourself best. You can let others
review it and comment on what is included and
what may be missing. When putting the resume
together, ask yourself questions about your work
history and experience.

Updated once a year or whenever your job
responsibilities change or significant
accomplishments occur—whichever comes first.

Think about your resume as a living thing that can grow
to reflect your own development. You may want to com-
pose a resume early in your job search just in case a "real"
offer comes along during your preparation phase. However, as you gain knowledge of the career or industry
you've targeted, update your resume to reflect your
greater knowledge. For example, you may find that entry-
level opportunities for advertising media buyers are soft

(not many available), but that openings for media plan-ners and analysts are wide open right now. If you have any experience in planning and analysis, you'll want to revise your resume to reflect this new interest and direction.

Also, because you will want to refine your resume as your job search progresses, it's probably best not to have 500 copies printed. Start with 15 or 20 copies on good quality white or off-white bond paper. Bond has a cotton rag content that makes the paper crisp. A 20– or 24–pound weight is appropriate; anything heavier may ap-pear to be extravagant. Don't use erasable bond or colored—other than an off-white or light gray—stock. You'll be approaching business and professional people who don't usually correspond on colored paper. You want your resume to stand out—but for the *right* reasons.

"Great minds have purposes. Others have wishes."

—WASHINGTON IRVING

While it is true that your resume should have a format, content, and appearance that accurately reflects your in-dividuality, it should also follow some general guidelines. By adhering to these guidelines, you'll be able to present yourself in the best possible light.

RESUME FORMATS

Although resumes come in several formats, the two types most widely used are:

The **chronological resume**, which lists various jobs in

reverse order, the current or most recent first. It usually includes a description of each job and a list of your accomplishments and basic responsibilities for each position.

The **functional resume** avoids, or plays down, the employment record. It describes your work experience and accomplishments in terms of functions. If, for example, you demonstrated the ability to plan and organize a community event, you could easily display that skill and supporting documentation in the functional resume, even though it may not be perceived as "work experience." It gives you more flexibility to highlight various work areas and then emphasize your experience and accomplishments in each functional area—particularly the one(s) in which you seek employment. This allows you to downplay certain work experiences and highlight others.

This format is a useful tool for people who are making major career changes or who have had significant gaps in employment. If you have had frequent job changes over a relatively short time period, they will not be as easily detected with a functional format. It is not that you are trying to hide anything from the prospective employer, but you don't want to be placed in the no pile without having an opportunity to explain the circumstances. The functional resume also provides the best format for emphasizing accomplishments outside of formal employment situations, such as experience gained in volunteer work, in school, and through hobbies. However, be aware that many employers really don't like this format, so exercise some caution when opting for this choice.

Both forms will be improved by listing accomplishments for each job or function.

Keep in mind that most employers still prefer the chronological resume. In addition, there are software programs available that allow an employer to scan-in pertinent data from the resume to make the screening process easier. These software programs are not designed to read the functional resume very well, if at all.

Many resumes contain a variety of categories of information. The three primary areas are an objective or summary of accomplishments, education, and experience. Other categories can include languages, awards, publications, professional memberships, military experience, etc. Examples of both types of resumes are included at the end of this section.

"The highest reward for a person's toil is not what they get for it, but what they become by it."

—JOHN RUSKIN

You always start your resume with your name, address, and home phone number at the top of the page and centered. Put your name in boldface type and go up one size. For example, if your resume is in 12–point type, put your name in 14 point. Do not put your address and phone number in boldface type. You want your name to stand out. If you are currently employed, do not put your work phone number on the resume. You should not be receiving job opportunity calls while someone else is paying you to work. In addition, your present employer may not be aware that you are looking for another job, and the caller may inadvertently divulge that information and there could be consequences. If your current employer has no objections to you receiving calls of this nature, include the work number in the cover letter.

Objective and Summary Statements

Since most resumes are read by busy people, it's to your advantage to get your key message across in a quick and interesting way very early.

The first thing most resume readers want to know is: "What kind of position are you looking for?" One way to answer this question is to begin the resume with a description of your objective. Examples:

A copyrighting, editing, or general advertising position within an agency or corporate department.

A technical training position that will take advantage of my three years' experience in summer jobs.

A marketing training position in the sales division of a small to medium-size company.

Remember that the objective needs to be somewhat specific to have any validity. In many cases, a summary of accomplishments makes more sense than an objective. In either case, it is not absolutely necessary to have either one on your resume.

Many graduates have more than one objective and therefore would accept more than one type of job offer. If this is the case, it's best to tailor separate resumes to fit each objective. Or you may prefer to leave the objective statement out of the resume and include it in your cover letter.

Because most employers also want to know what kind of job candidate you are and what you can actually do, a summary statement (following your objective statement if placed in your resume) can answer this question. A summary statement presents the broad picture of who you are and what an employer can expect from you. The recommendation would be to put the summary statement in the resume with the objective statement in the cover letter. Some resume readers won't bother reading further if the document has no summary statement—it saves them time and speeds their judgment process. Remember, many resumes only receive a fifteen-to-thirty-second scan before a decision is made. The objective statement and summary statement must always be in agreement. Examples:

Objective statement in cover letter	*Summary statement in resume*
An accounting position with a Big Six firm in the Northeast.	An organized, detail-oriented business school graduate who works well under pressure, with an accounting major and summer experience in mid-size New York City firms. Solid accomplishments in cost accounting and budget planning.
A laboratory position with a bio-engineering firm in California.	An energetic, highly motivated master's graduate in biochemistry with four years of experience as a laboratory assistant manager. Graduate fellowship with the National Academy of Sciences.

| An environmental engineer in an international organization. | A results-oriented engineering graduate with a minor in environmental studies; worked for three summers with Jacques Cousteau studying underwater life. |

Education

Most recent graduates' work experience consists of several summer jobs that lasted only a few months and required rather basic skills. Because these experiences aren't the major thing they have to "sell" a prospective employer, many choose to put their *Education* section before their *Experience* section in the resume. A good rule of thumb to follow: if your full-time work experience is less than five years and you have a four-year degree, list your education first. If you have worked for five years or more, list the experience first.

SEARCH TIP

There's nothing that compensates better for a lack of experience than enthusiasm.

List your educational history in a reverse chronology, beginning with your latest (or anticipated) degree. The only exception is that you always list your highest degree first. For example, a master's degree would be listed first followed by your second bachelor's degree, even if you received the second bachelor's degree more recently. Recent graduates should include any experiences they've had during their education that corroborate their ability to fulfill the position for which they are applying. If you did a substantial research project, describe it. If you have taken courses that support your job ambitions but are not a part of your major, specify what you learned and how it will contribute to your competency on the job.

While these are part of your education, language and computer skills may warrant a listing under a separate category.

If you acquired a Grade Point Average of 3.5 or better, include this in the *Education* section of your resume. If your overall average wasn't that great but was much better, for example, in your senior year, indicate this. Some employers, notably financial institutions and consulting firms, insist on seeing a GPA before they will seriously consider a candidate. Once you have been out of school for a few years and have gained some experience, your GPA will lose its significance and should be removed from your resume.

Some career counselors say that if you attended a college or university other than the one from which you graduated, you should list this school second in your *Education* section. However, unless it was involved in study abroad or was focused on a discipline other than your degree, it probably won't have much value in the minds of prospective employers. Once you have a bachelor's degree, your associate's degree has less relevance for your career objectives. The exception is if the two-year degree is in a technical discipline that differs from your four-year degree. For example, an AS in Electronics and a BS in Business should both be included on the resume, but an

AS in Business and a BS in Business should only show the BS in Business on the resume.

Include any special honors, courses, or experiences that relate to your career goal. Extracurricular, public service, and volunteer activities are important and should be included, either here or in a separate category with an appropriate heading. They portray the breadth of your interests and demonstrate that you were not in school just to study . . . or just to play. Fraternity, sorority, and club memberships can be included under your *Education* section or, if they are numerous, in a separate *Activities* section. But emphasize your leadership positions under *Experience*.

Do not list high school, prep school, etc. under *Education*. If that is all you have, consider omitting this section from your resume.

Experience

This section identifies the positions you have held and your responsibilities and accomplishments during each tenure. Use action verbs in the present tense for current position—*managing, leading, training*, etc.—and past tense for former positions—*created, led, organized, presented*, etc.—to describe your activities and achievements as dynamically as possible. Include all your positions, paid and unpaid, including volunteer, part-time, internships, and work-study positions. You don't need to write in full sentences, and you can use bullets to highlight your significant accomplishments.

When listing dates of employment, use only years, not months or days. Let's look at the following example. John was laid off on January 2, 1993 and diligently looked for another job. Frustration became his companion until he finally secured a new position on December 21, 1994. Mary was caught in a downsizing on December 27, 1993. She went to a New Year's Eve party and met an individual who was looking to hire someone with Mary's skills. She started on January 4, 1994. Now if we do the calculations, John was unemployed for a total of 724 days and Mary was unemployed for seven days. And yet, by using only the years on their respective resumes, the dates are the same for both individuals.

"Do not wish to be anything but what you are, and try to be that perfectly."
—St. Francis de Sales

Other Categories

As was stated earlier, you may have experiences, skills, or other backgrounds that don't fit neatly into *Experience* or *Education*. Create appropriate titles for these areas. For example, if you speak and/or write a language other than English, say so and specify your level of competence. It should either be fluent (read, write, and speak) or conversational. Don't list it if you can't demonstrate it. If you are skilled in the use of a computer or word processor, include this information—along with the programs you have mastered. If you have had articles published in recognized journals, then these should be listed. The potential categories go on and on, but be careful not to have too many.

Do not include:

Any mention of your age, race, religion, gender, national origin, marital status, or number of children. This information is not work-related, and it could be used to screen you out. The courts have ruled this information may be the basis for discrimination, and is therefore illegal for an employer to ask. Don't offer it to them.

Your physical description or mention of your height, weight, or general health. Any criminal past or reference to "no criminal record," as one candidate indicated on his resume.

Any listing of references—or even a mention. It's assumed that most people seeking a job have people who will recommend them. Wait until you're asked for your references. It is unnecessary to write "References Available Upon Request" at the end of the resume.

Any reference to salary earned in earlier positions or salary requirements for the job sought.

The word resume at the top of the document. Almost everyone knows what one looks like.

Resumes and Cover Letters

Your first objective, of course, is a face-to-face meeting with the interviewer or contact. From this perspective, sending the resume is a compromise: it's "you"—only not in person. Also, since it's a standardized document, it can't be an exact match for every situation. When asked for your resume, always send a well-written and tailor-made cover letter with it. The cover letter becomes your customizing tool—introducing your resume with a particular focus, addressing your job objectives and, if known, the specific needs of the reader. Highlight your relevant educational and work experiences to help the reader recognize the connection to the position in his or her organization. The cover letter is examined in greater detail later.

Writing the Resume

Armed with the advice on the preceding pages, you can now write your resume. Use the exercise sheets provided on the following pages to develop a chronological resume first. Then, if you wish, use that to construct the one with a functional format.

"Chance favors the prepared mind."
—LOUIS PASTEUR

Don't get discouraged if you don't create a masterpiece right away. It may well take you several drafts before you have a document you're comfortable with—a resume that creates as accurate and positive an impression of you as possible.

Remember, the resume is only a tool in your job search. But it is a vital tool. You'll be presenting it to prospective employers, personnel counselors, and various contacts you'll meet in your job-hunting process. To be most useful to you, your resume has to make you feel good about it. If you're not satisfied with your early results, keep working. Get advice from someone you respect. If you're still at your college or university, ask a professional in your career office for advice and analysis. You should be pleased with the resume you come up with as your final product. If it's right for you, you'll be proud to present it as your personal advertisement.

One other thought to consider before you embark upon this task. Not all work history needs to be part of the resume. The "filler" job that lasted six months and served only to earn money to pay the bills need not be included in the resume. It *does* need to be listed on a job application. Failure to do so could result in termination. Also, your work history should not go back any further than about twenty years. There usually is little relevance to experience that is farther back.

CHRONOLOGICAL RESUME FORMAT

Name _____
Address _____
City, State, Zip _____
Telephone Number _____

OBJECTIVE (Remember, this is optional)

_____
_____

SUMMARY OF ACCOMPLISHMENTS

_____
_____

EDUCATION

Degree and Major Field: _____
School: _____
Location (City, State): _____
Year of Graduation: _____
GPA, Activities, Organizations: _____

WORK EXPERIENCE

Company: _____
Location (City, State): _____
Dates Employed: _____
Job Title: _____
Responsibilities: _____

Accomplishments: _____
_____
_____

Company: _____
Location (City, State): _____
Dates Employed: _____
Job Title: _____
Responsibilities: _____

Accomplishments: _____
_____
_____

FUNCTIONAL RESUME FORMAT

Name _____

Address _____

City, State, Zip _____

Telephone Number _____

OBJECTIVE (Remember, this is optional)

_____

_____

SUMMARY OF ACCOMPLISHMENTS

_____

_____

MAJOR ACCOMPLISHMENTS

Functional Area: _____

Functional Area: _____

Functional Area: _____

Functional Area: _____

EDUCATION

Degree and Major Field: _____

School: _____

Location (City, State): _____

Year of Graduation: _____

GPA, Activities, Organizations: _____

WORK EXPERIENCE

Company: _____

Location (City, State): _____

Job Title: _____

Dates Employed: _____

Company: _____

Location (City, State): _____

Job Title: _____

Dates Employed: _____

CHRONOLOGICAL MODEL RESUMES—FORMAT #1

Beth A. Owens
196 Prospect Street
Madison, NJ 07940
(201) 555–8702

Professional Objective
An entry-level position in international banking

Education
BA International Relations/Political Science (Cum Laude) Colgate University, Hamilton, NY. 3.5 GPA. 1995. Additional courses in computer sciences, French, and Spanish.

Graduate-level courses in marketing, corporate finance, intermediate accounting, and federal taxation. University of Hartford, Summer 1995.

Honors
Dean's List six out of eight semesters; Phi Eta Sigma, Freshman Honor Society; Pi Sigma Alpha, National Political Science Honor Society; Selected Member, Geneva Study Group. Intensive study in European politics, organizations, banking, and trade relations. Fall 1993.

Experience
Research Assistant, Psychology Department, Colgate University. Assisted in coding and analyzing data from various studies. Results pending publication. Winter 1994–1995.

Bank Teller, Midlantic North Bank, West Paterson, NJ. Managed and processed financial transactions. Gained knowledge of banking procedures. Summer 1993.

Manager (Part-time), Village Shop, a women's clothing store, Wayne, NJ. Supervised employees, managed daily financial transactions, and developed public relations skills. Summers, school holidays, 1992–1995.

Waitress/Hostess, Oliver's Restaurant, Yarmouth, MA. Developed public relations skills. Facilitated the flow of business and handled customer complaints. Summer 1990.

Co-Curricular Activities
Writer, The Colgate News. Researched and wrote feature articles as well as regular sports coverage.

Dorm Representative, West Hall Dormitory, Colgate University. Organized various student activities.

CHRONOLOGICAL MODEL RESUMES—FORMAT #2

Martha A. Evans
241 Huntington Street
Brentwood, NY 11717
(516) 555-7409

Objective: Seeking a position in computer programming with opportunities for advancement in systems analysis.

Education: **BS Computer Science** Monmouth College, West Long Branch, NJ 07764. Projected Graduation: May 1996. Overall GPA 3.7; GPA in Major 3.8.

Experience: Employed during Spring and Fall Intercessions through the following agencies:

1993 to present
Data Entry Temporaries, Parsippany, NJ
Data Entry Clerk—served in a temporary capacity for various client companies including: Warner Lambert, BASF. Responsibilities included: data entry and general clerical duties.

1993 to present
Hartshorn Services, Parsippany, NJ
Receptionist and Clerical Assistant—served in a temporary capacity for various client companies including: Hertz, Citicorp, Metem Corporation, Daily Record. Responsibilities included: receptionist and general clerical skills.

1991 to present
Office Force, Cedar Knolls, NJ
Data Entry and Clerical Assistant—served in a temporary capacity for various client companies including: Fireman's Fund Insurance Co., Office Force. Responsibilities included: Data entry, general clerical skills, entrusted with running the office for Office Force during relocation to New Jersey.

Specialized Skills:

Software	Hardware
PASCAL, COBOL, GW BASIC, C	BTI,
IBM 360/370 Assembler	Perkin-Elmer 3250XP
Rockwell R6502 Microprocessor	AIM 65 Microcomputer
VI Editor	AT&T PC

Activities:
President, Computer Science Honor Society, 1993–present.
Member, Computer Science Honor Society, 1992.
Member, Mathematics Honor Society, 1993–present.
Member, Monmouth College Honors Program, 1991–present.
Member, Gamma Sigma National Service Sorority, 1991–1994.

Ronald F. Johnson
123 Main Street
Norwalk, CT 06851
203-555-4982

SUMMARY

Over five years experience in human resource management with skills in recruitment, employee relations and compensation and benefits.

EXPERIENCE

1990–Present *The Hartsdale Corporation*, Norwalk, CT. A small manufacturing company involved with injection molding and product assembly.

Manager of Human Resources—responsible for the management of all human resources functions including staffing, performance reviews, compensation and benefits, and employee relations.

Created a behavioral interviewing staffing program that resulted in a decrease in employee turnover by 100%.

Developed a comprehensive performance appraisal process that focused on performance measures for all 37 employees.

Researched and implemented a new benefits program that saved the company over $100,000 in the first year.

EDUCATION

BA Human Resource Management University of Bridgeport, Bridgeport, CT. 1990.

MBA Management Fairfield University, Fairfield, CT (in process).

FUNCTIONAL MODEL RESUME

Raymond F. Adriance

2912 West Jefferson Street
Summit, CO 80221
(303) 555-7122

Job Goal: Professional or management position in training function of a growth-oriented organization.

Summary: As training assistant, coordinated the development and delivery of company management and supervisory development programs.

Major Accomplishments:

Research and Needs Analysis
Developed management audit to assess strengths and training deficits of supervisory and management personnel. Designed data collection system to utilize current computer capabilities in company. Assessed long-range manpower requirements resulting in allocation of $750,000 additional funding for recruitment, hiring, and training.

Program Design, Development, and Delivery
Coordinated development of customized training programs using in-house staff. Trained over 60 managers in "How to Manage More Effectively." Chosen as keynote speaker for area conference on Training and Development.

Supervision and Administration
Supervised seven professional staff and three support persons. Developed and monitored $1,000,000 training budget. Effectively recruited and trained five new program specialists.

Work History:

1991–Present Coordinator, Human Resources, Allstate Bank, Littleton, CO.

1988–1991 Administrative Assistant, Littleton Chamber of Commerce, Littleton, CO.

1985–1988 U.S. Army, Sgt. E-5, Honorable Discharge.

Education: **BS Business Administration** University of Colorado at Denver, Denver, CO.

Anticipated Graduation: May 1996.

Related Professional Experience: Member, Rocky Mountain Chapter, American Society for Training and Development.

Remember, most organizations prefer the chronological resume, but use the format that serves your purpose most effectively. There is one other format that can also be used. A comprehensive letter that summarizes your experience and education can be used in place of a resume as a starting point. You will still need to prepare a resume using one of the formats described previously. The major reason to use the letter format is to get the attention of a senior-level person in an organization. In most organizations, if you send a resume with a standard cover letter, the administrative assistants have been told to send all of those inquiries to the human resources department. A letter looks like another piece of correspondence for the manager and will probably end up on his or her desk. A letter format is useful as a way to tell people that you may be entering the job market and asking them to let you know if they learn of any opportunities.

Resume preparation is a lot of work, but if you want to take control of your career, you need to plan and prepare properly in order to bring about success. Review the resume checklist in the next paragraph after you have prepared your first draft and before you send out your first resume.

Resume Checklist

Remember, on the resume you don't have to tell the truth, the whole truth, and nothing but the truth, but you can't lie. What this means is that you don't need to include every job you have ever had. Look at your job titles; are they truly descriptive of the position? If not, how would you change the title to describe the job more accurately? What you can't do is elevate the title. For example, if your title is Assistant Accounting Clerk, you cannot put on the resume that you were the Chief Financial Officer.

Don't lie on your resume. It is too easy to verify things like places of employment and degrees.

Remember what we said earlier. Put your resume up on the wall, step back ten feet and ask yourself this question: "Does it look inviting to read?" What is your answer now? Will it keep you out of the no pile?

Resume Do's and Don'ts

Here is a handy reference list of things to examine on your resume.

DO

Present yourself accurately and positively.

Include only enough information to interest the reader.

Have someone else proofread your resume before it is printed.

Limit your resume to no more than two pages, except in very unusual circumstances.

Use type that is small enough to allow more text on a page without looking crowded, but large enough so that it can be easily read.

Include a summary statement.

Include your most important accomplishments and responsibilities.

Cover all time periods in your employment history.

Use an attractive layout and first-class paper for a pleasing professional appearance.

DON'T

Include desired or current salary.

Include references or even state that they will be available upon request.

Use long, complicated sentences, jargon, or buzz words, unless they are commonly used.

Allude to objectives for which you are clearly not qualified.

Neglect to provide a complete employment history and description of responsibilities and scope for all positions.

As you review your resume, check it against the following points:

1. Is it readable, with varied use of short paragraphs, bullets, and white space?

2. Is it interesting? Would you want to read it if you were the prospective employer?

3. Is it clear? Would an employer know within thirty seconds to one minute what type of job you want and why you are qualified?

4. Is it professional? Is it letter perfect, with no misspellings, typos, or smudges?

5. Is it comprehensive without being exhaustive?

6. Have you quantified some of your accomplishments?

7. Is it accurate and honest?

8. Does it invite the reader to find out more about you?

9. Did you use action verbs to describe accomplishments?

10. Do your accomplishment statements support your stated job objective?

11. When you read over your resume, are you impressed? Do you feel a sense of pride and accomplishment?

12. Would you hire yourself?

13. What color paper are you using and what type fonts are used? The paper should be white or off-white or perhaps light gray, and of good quality. Make sure you use one of the good basic fonts— CG Times, Times New Roman, Ariel, etc. rather than Pica or Elite, which look as if they came off a typewriter.

14. Last but certainly not least, update your resume annually or whenever your job changes (whichever comes first). Even if you are not actively in the job market, you never know when you might be, and keeping your resume current will be to your advantage.

CHAPTER 5

Assessing Today's Job Market

Looking for your first career position after college is a lot like selling a new product. In this case, *you* are the product! To market yourself, you have to learn all you can about your customers (your potential employers), where they're located, and what they will pay you for your skills. You also need to know how to appeal to them to your maximum advantage. To develop this *marketing*—or job search—strategy, you should be able to answer the following questions:

What kinds of companies or industries are interested in your skills?

What is the title of the person who can actually hire you? Do you need to be interviewed by the vice-president for finance? The regional sales manager? The human resources director? Someone else?

Where are the firms that interest you located? Do they have local, regional, or national offices? Which office should you approach to get the job you want? Who is the individual you have to see to get that position?

How can you best make contact with these *prospect* firms? Through your personal network? Search firms? Blanket distribution of resumes? Or through direct contact with the company by letter and telephone follow-up?

Which of your qualities (education, experience, skills, personality, etc.) will make you especially interesting to these firms?

What is the general salary range for the position you seek? How does that range relate to the salaries for entry-level positions in other types of business, and for other types of careers?

At the beginning of your job search, it's important to make a realistic assessment of the situation. First, there are limited job opportunities. That should not come as a surprise to you unless you haven't spoken to friends and acquaintances who have graduated in the past few years. Many organizations, both large and small, have been going through extended periods of downsizing. Because of this, employers are now looking at candidates somewhat differently than in days gone by. They want to hire only the *best* people. It's not that they didn't have high standards before, it's just that supply exceeds demand and it has become a buyer's market. Employers can be more selective. So what is your competitive advantage?

Kevin Harrington, director of the Career Services Office at the Harvard Graduate School of Education, indicates that "many students entering the job market have unrealistic expectations of what is available, what they have been trained for, and what level of compensation they will receive. In addition, many students fail to improve the situation because they don't do enough networking and they don't gather enough information and intelligence about the market place and targeted companies. Doing these things will increase the probability of success tremendously."

The tighter job market and the more selective employer have impacted starting salaries. It used to be that you could receive a starting salary higher than your counterparts who graduated a few years before you. That is no longer the case. The starting salaries have remained somewhat constant over the past four years and that is not expected to change in the near future.

What Limitations Exist for You?

What is the size of the market you're approaching? Are you limiting your market to a local or regional area? What are the trade-offs in broadening your market . . . or restricting it? Do you have enough education and experience to be competitive? Are you willing to work hard? These assessments are essential to designing a realistic marketing effort that will produce the results you seek.

It's essential to conduct some research before you make contact in the marketplace. By doing this homework, you'll have current knowledge of relevant industry trends and company reputations. These are important pluses, because in all your contacts with potential employers, it will be clear to each interviewer, phone contact, and recipient of your letters that your interest in the company is backed by true initiative and solid preparation.

RESEARCH IS THE KEY

As a job seeker, you need to ask yourself this question: "How well prepared am I to enter the job search process?" The issue is not as simple as it may sound. In reality, the job search process today for most entry-level college graduates is time consuming, energy draining, and often frustrating. The candidates who mentally prepare themselves to face those challenges and hurdles are the ones with the best success rate.

A major key to that success is the research component. Let's look at all the factors pertinent to that process in the following checklist.

Self—prior to any research on a particular employer, you need a keen awareness of your:

interests

abilities

values

desired lifestyle

Each of these factors is within your total control and should have been validated prior to your embarking upon your first job. If not, then you are bound to be dissatisfied.

Situation— some of the more external factors you must research and evaluate include:

the economy and the labor market

your desired geographic location

the influence of significant others

the level of education required

While some of these factors are beyond your control, they must be realistically assessed.

The next step will be to conduct research on the sector of work you wish to enter, that is, the industry and its potential employers. A checklist of helpful information to research includes:

historic and recent trends in the industry and specific employers

noteworthy employers within the industry

the specific organization(s):

history, size, and growth

its profitability

its products and services

the financial history and current status

the organizational structure and its key management

the company philosophy and culture

any recent changes in the company structure

changes in product or service lines

geographic area job trends

How Important Is Researching Employers?

Many job seekers put a tremendous amount of time and effort into self-assessment efforts, preparation of their resumes, and interview techniques. While all of these efforts are of great importance, if job seekers stop there, they are putting themselves in a disadvantageous position for several reasons.

First, both job seeker and employer have much at stake in the selection process. Neither wants the choice to be an inappropriate one. Each is anxious to see that the best match between the job and the candidate is made. According to Ed Ryan, president of Marketing Personnel Research, Inc., a Chicago-based worldwide consulting firm specializing in productivity improvement by selection and management of talented people for all positions within an organization, "Making a bad hiring decision can cost an employer up to three times the annual compensation of the position, in terms of replacement costs, lost opportunity costs, etc."

The research process is important to the candidate validation process. Each candidate needs to be satisfied that the type of position, organization, location, and other details are compatible with his or her interests, values, and desired lifestyle. Also, the most competitive candidates spend many hours conducting research on those employers they plan to target in their job search. This will certainly give them an advantage over those who under-utilize this aspect of the process.

Laura Volz has spent a major part of her career in human resources and corporate recruiting with two major insurance companies. In addressing this very issue, she says, "The best candidate I ever interviewed was totally prepared. She had done extensive research on the company, had strong knowledge of the insurance industry, knew the company's strategic direction, and came with a list of questions. She had a sincere interest in the company. She was focused not just on finding a job, she wanted a career and wanted to maximize her potential."

"Things may come to those who wait, but only the things left by those who act."
—ABRAHAM LINCOLN

Of even greater importance is the priority this process holds for the employer. Key hiring criteria for all employers include the candidate's level of interest and enthusiasm. If the candidate takes the time and makes the effort to gain a reasonable understanding of the employer's business and organization in general, he or she will project this initiative during the interview. Employers are interested in hearing what the candidates can and will do for their organizations, not just what the candidates expect from them. A comment too often seen on candidates' interview evaluations goes something like this: "It was obvious that this candidate did not take the time or have the interest to read or learn about our organization, its philosophy, or mission." The result—a rejection letter.

Libraries Hold One of the Keys

The beauty of using your university's library or, for that matter, most any public library, is that you can both assess and access the marketplace in one visit. Let's first look at major publications aimed at providing useful information about organizations that you will need to know in order to:

- determine if it meets your career aspirations
- amass a knowledge base about the employer that will help make your job search and interview more competitive.

These resources are a combination of both hard copy directions and electronic/computer programs. Many people now have access to the Internet, and a lot of this information may be accessed on your personal computer from the comfort of your home.

Hard Copy

Employer's Annual Report— This is must reading, because it details the employer's entire financial picture for the previous year, its mission and goals, products and services, and its operating philosophy. You can often learn about the organizational structure as well.

Employer's Recruitment Literature— Along with the annual report, many employers have recruitment literature that they will provide to prospective employees. If you have time to read only two publications, these are the key ones. It's important to remember that both of these publications are products of the individual organization and therefore may carry certain favorable biases toward the employer. Also, there will be no comparative data with other organizations or against a particular industry. The recruitment brochure will detail specific job types that every candidate needs to know and, if read discriminantly, will give solid clues on issues to discuss in the interview. One employer's brochure stated, "Our strategy is to use a team approach . . ." and "We are totally committed to providing quality service . . ." Another employer's brochure included, "Our employees are action-oriented and encouraged and rewarded for being creative." Any serious job candidate should be able to use these clues effectively during the interview and even earlier—for example, in the cover letter when requesting an interview.

"We are continually faced by great opportunities brilliantly disguised as insoluble problems."

—ANONYMOUS

Index of research sources

There are a number of business directories that can be useful in planning your strategy to locate the right position. The directories listed below can be found at most public, college, university, and business libraries. In many urban areas, local directories are published by the Chamber of Commerce and governmental agencies.

Before using any directory, however, read its Preface and Table of Contents. This will save you time and indicate the most efficient way to locate the information you need. This is only a representative list and is not intended to be viewed as all-inclusive.

Guide to American Directories (B. Klein Publications, P.O. Box 8503, Coral Springs, FL 33065). A listing and description of 6,000 directories with more than 300 major industrial, professional, and mercantile classifications.

Encyclopedia of Associations, *Volume 1* (National Organizations of the United States, Gale Research Company, Book Tower, Detroit, MI 48266). A guide to 14,000 national organizations of all types, purposes, and interests. Gives names and headquarters addresses; telephone numbers; chief officials; number of members; staffs and chapters; descriptions of memberships, programs, and activities. Includes lists of special committees and departments, publications, and three-year convention schedules. The publication is cross-indexed. It is also useful in locating placement committees that can help you learn of specific job openings in your field of interest; getting membership lists of individuals in order to develop personal contacts; and learning where and when conferences are being held.

Directory of Corporate Affiliations (National Register Publishing Company, Inc., 5201 Old Orchard Road, Skokie, IL 60076). Provides detailed information on "who owns whom" as a result of mergers and acquisitions. Includes companies listed on the New York Stock Exchange, the American Stock Exchange, the *Fortune 500* and others—a total of 4,000 parent company listings. This directory is useful when seeking detailed information on the corporate structure of a parent company or for a company not listed in other directories because it is a subsidiary division or affiliate.

The Career Guide: Dun's Employment Opportunities Directory (Dun and Bradstreet Information Services, 99 Church Street, New York, NY 10007). Employers are listed alphabetically, and each entry includes a list of educational and experience specialties the company generally hires. Indexes help locate companies by geographic areas, industry, and disciplines hired.

Moody's Manuals (Moody's Investor Services). Information obtained from company reports, proxy statements, and regulatory reports form this eight-volume set.

Standard and Poor's Register of Corporations, Directors, and Executives (Standard and Poor, Inc., 345 Hudson Street, New York, NY 10014). Standard and Poor's (S&P) Register includes an alphabetical listing of more than 55,000 corporations, of which more than 75 percent are privately owned. Information is indexed by standard industrial classification (SIC) codes, geographic locations, and corporate family.

ValueLine Investment Survey. A quarterly publication that gives you an overview by industry. It provides one-page financial and statistical reviews of organizations and industries, including projections for future growth and development. A great publication for both comparing organizations and projecting trends among employers.

Standard and Poor's Industry Surveys. A quarterly publication whose focus is by industry type, that is, publishing, retail, petroleum, etc. Several pages are devoted to each group. It also contains charts and graphs comparing individual employer's operating revenues, net income, debt capital ratio, etc. within each industry.

Polk's World Bank Directory—North American Edition (U.S., Canada, Mexico, Central America, and Caribbean), (R. L. Polk Company, 2001 Elm Hill Pike, P.O. Box 1340, Nashville, TN 37202). A detailed listing of banks, other financial institutions, and government agencies by address. Also includes a geographic indexing with maps, names, and titles of officers. It can be useful in researching financial corporations and government agencies.

A. M. Best's Insurance Reports, Property, and Casualty and **A. M. Best's Insurance Reports, Life and Health** (A. M. Best Company, Ambest Road, Oldwick, NJ 08858). These publications provide in-depth analyses, operating statistics, financial data, and officers of more than 1,300 major stock and mutual property-casualty insurance companies, over 2,000 smaller mutual companies, 300 casualty companies operating in Canada, and 1,250 individual life and health company reports in addition to a summary of 600 smaller life and health companies.

Electronic Resources

Electronic formats of information can save hours of research time. Many libraries buy expensive CD-ROM products and have access to on-line databases. CD-ROM searching is generally free of charge, but customers usually must pay the cost of on-line searching. If you are not experienced in this area, get some advice and direction, because the learning experience could get to be very expensive without yielding much value. There are many electronic resources available; a few are listed here.

In a job search you need to be the champion, the advocate, and the salesperson of "you."

Dun's Electronic Business Directory (Dun and Bradstreet Information Services). An on-line directory containing information on more than 8 million businesses and professionals, with 15 broad business categories. It is updated quarterly and is usually available at libraries through Dialog Information Services on File 515.

Dun's Million Dollar CD-ROM Collection (Dun and Bradstreet Information Services). This includes three databases that focus on different markets: large companies, mid-level companies, and service-industry and public administration companies with annual revenues of at least $1 million. Information on the top 160,000 public and private U.S. companies is also available through Dialog on File 517.

ABI/Inform Ondisc (Data Courier, Inc.). Updated monthly, this CD-ROM product contains citations and abstracts for articles found in 800 business journals.

Business Index—Public Edition (Information Access Co.). It covers more than 700 business, management, and trade journals, including 50 local business periodicals.

Business Periodicals Index (H. W. Wilson Co.). While its periodical coverage isn't as extensive as other directories, it has gained a good reputation for thorough indexing of business subjects.

The Wall Street Journal Index (Dow Jones and Co.). This index, also available on-line and on CD-ROM, provides abstracts and coverage of all articles in *The Wall Street Journal*. It is divided into two sections: corporate news and general news.

American Business Disc (American Business Information). Information is compiled from more than 5,000 telephone directories, annual reports, and chambers of commerce membership and directors lists to produce this CD-ROM database of 10 million businesses nationwide.

Company ProFile (Information Access Co.). Offered on CD-ROM, it is a directory of information on more than 150,000 private and public companies. You can retrieve information on the top 100 companies ranked by sales in an industry, city, or state by merely typing in the SIC code or the geographic area.

With the fast-paced changes in electronic technology, additional sources and resources will continue to become available and grow rapidly throughout the rest of this decade and beyond.

Other Data Sources

In addition to the information available above, you can gain valuable knowledge through a variety of other sources. These include:

Corporate 10K Reports, available from all public companies, provide financial and historic information about a corporation. May be requested from each company's treasurer's office, public relations, or public information office. May also be available from public accounting firms, banks, and business, college, and university libraries.

Prospectus—as a part of every public stock offering, a company's prospectus includes financial and historic data as well as information on the firm's directors, officers, and "insiders."

The Annual Report (public companies only)—in addition to the balance sheet and the auditor's report, these documents also contain a letter from the chairperson (and/or president) that usually reflects the firm's personality, well-being, and direction.

In addition to the preceding research resources, there are many industry, Chamber of Commerce, and *Fortune 500* directories, trade journals, annual reports, and papers that may be found at your local business, college, university, and public libraries.

You may also find valuable corporate and industry information in the following:

Occupational Outlook Handbook

Directory of American Firms Operating in Foreign Countries

Congressional Directory

The following business-oriented magazines may also prove helpful:

Barron's

BusinessWeek

Business World

Forbes

Fortune

Inc.

Money

Nation's Business

Success

Accessing the Marketplace

The paradigm is rapidly changing for college and university career development and placement offices, as reflected by the shift in name changes at many schools. The word *placement* is rapidly disappearing, and the more common title is now *career services*. The major mission today of career services offices is focused on the career counseling and planning activities of self-assessment, individual counseling, career courses, internship coordination, etc. Activities like on-campus recruiting, career fairs, and resume referral programs, while still in existence and basically viable, are not nearly as prominent as in past decades. One main reason for this is the growth of accessing employment opportunities through the electronic media, available wherever a computer can be found—the university or public library, dorm room, or in the job seeker's own home. It is not unrealistic to suggest that by the turn of the century, most job seekers will be independently accessing employment opportunities using computers and other electronic media. Let's look at some of the major programs that assist with the process today.

SEARCH TIP

If you don't believe in yourself no one else will believe in you or your potential either.

The Internet

This is a network of networks that is accessible not only from public and university libraries but from your own computer. It allows you to connect to resources all over the world. This includes all of the electronic accessing methods mentioned earlier plus many new and emerging programs specific to job listing and advertisements. It is important to note that these systems are very much in their infancy and there has been little opportunity thus far to research outcomes. Also, new programs are being created, probably monthly, so you need to make inquiries continually into what programs are available.

Once on an Internet system, you will need to seek out a *Gopher*. A Gopher is a software program that provides menu access to selected resources on the Internet and on the local network. Each institution and/or public library defines what resources to include. Here are a few of the better known current systems:

Online Career Center (OCC)
3125 Dandy Trail
Suite 3
Indianapolis, IN 46214
317-293-6499
FAX 317-293-6692
Internet: gopher.occ.com
http://www.occ.com/occ/
E-mail resume to: occ-resumes@occ.com.

The non-profit Online Career Center contains searchable job postings from over 200 companies. Potential employers include industrial, corporate, institutional, healthcare, governmental, and educational organizations. The OCC provides a database to search for jobs by city, state, regions of the U.S., or a key word. Job postings are current and provide a job description, salary, application process, qualifications, and contact person. 10–12,000 jobs are currently listed.

Resumes can be entered for free—18–20,000 resumes are on the system now; the resume database can be searched at no charge by an employer with Internet access. Resumes stay on the system for 3 months and, if renewed, can be on indefinitely. For those that cannot e-mail, the Online Resume Service will place a resume on the OCC for $10.

FedWorld (Federal Job Openings)
Internet: telnet fedworld.doc.gov
http://www.fedworld.gov
ftp.fedworld.gov
modem 703-321-8020

FedWorld is run by the National Technical Information Service (NTIS) and is a gateway to many federal bulletin board systems. In order to use FedWorld, you must register your name, address, and password with NTIS. This database allows you to search for jobs by state, by region of the U.S., or internationally. The listings provide job titles, job locations, contact persons, and a listing of the necessary forms to submit. Choose menu option (J) Federal Job Openings.

Career Connections
5150 El Camino Real
Suite D33
Los Altos, CA 94022
voice 415-903-5800
FAX 415-903-5848
modem 415-903-5840 (2400 bps), 415-903-5815
   (9600-14.4 bps)
E-mail: postmaster@career.com
Internet:
   telnet://career.com for professional listings
   telnet://college.career.com for new college graduate
      listings
   telnet://jobfair.career.com for CyberFairs
   (virtual job fairs for companies)
World Wide Web: http://www.career.com

Career Connections is an on-line interactive employment network. There is no charge for candidates to fill in a profile on-line (the system generates the resume itself and creates a private password/e-mail/profile account) and access 1500–2000 international job listings. Companies pay to advertise their open positions, mainly professional and managerial jobs. This is a fast-growing system taking full advantage of the latest technology. Career Connections is receiving 580–1,000 resumes a day, and 4500–5500 requests a day on the Web site to view and respond to positions. You can search the system by company, discipline, or geographic area. There is also a specific category directed at new graduates.

One of the key issues for the recent college graduate job seeker today is the breadth and diversity of strategies that must be used to be successful in obtaining the position of choice. While there is not specific research to pinpoint success rates of any one individual strategy, most career practitioners suggest that by only using a single strategy your hit ratio will only be 10 to 15 percent. Therefore, to be successful, you should use *seven* to *ten* different job strategies. Remember, the proactive person gets the job.

Computerized Job and Resume Data Banks

Another emerging technology-based employment resource is the computerized data banks. For the most part, these are commercial ventures, whereby a fee is charged to the candidate, the employer, or both. These services are also so new to the marketplace that little is known about the outcome or success rates. It does appear from early information that many candidates and employers are participating and that it is a growing job search strategy. Some of the more promoted ones include:

JobWeb
Http://www.jobweb.org

Career planning and employment info, job-search articles and tips, job listings, and company information for college students, recent graduates and alumni. Sponsored by the National Association of Colleges and Employers (NACE), formerly known as the College Placement Council (CPC). It is a comprehensive resource for employers who hire college graduates and for students and alumni in the job search. There is a modest fee for the employer, but none for the candidate.

JOBTRAK
1990 Westwood Boulevard
Suite 260
Los Angeles, CA 90025
800-999-8725, 310-474-3377
FAX 310-475-7912
http://www.jobtrak.com

Over 300 college and university career centers pay to post their job opportunities, employer profiles, and job hunting tips on-line for a 2–4 week period. Currently processing over 500 new job listings each day. Over 150,000 employers have utilized this service, which enables them to target their job order to students and alumni at their specific choice of campuses.

University Placement Service
618-453-1047

Entry level (maybe 10% alums). There is a fee of $16 for resume referral to a potential employer; also has a Hotline service for $25, with 7 counselors in different areas.

Job Bank USA
1420 Spring Hill Road
Suite 480

McLean, VA 22102
800-296-1872, 703-847-1706
FAX 703-847-1494

Job Bank USA serves over 2,000 employer clients with a job seekers' data bank of over 25,000 resumes. Cost is $125 for 1 year enrollment and a Career Fitness Kit of books, software, a discount card, catalog, newsletter, and other resources for effective job search and career management in the 1990's. 65% of the database is currently employed.

SkillSearch
104 Woodmont Boulevard
Suite 306
Nashville, TN 37205
800-258-6641
FAX 615-834-9453

This organization works with approximately 60 alumni groups and is directed at college graduates with two years of work experience. The client fee is $65 for two years. Currently there are over 500 employers and 40,000 candidates in the data bank.

Career Net Online
1788 Wyrick Avenue
San Jose, CA 95124
800-392-7967, 408-269-3910
FAX 408-269-5608

Individual job seeker pays $42 to have profile or "Mini-Resume" included in a searchable on-line database (50% currently employed). Same profile or "Mini-Resume" will also be mailed to 3,000 employers and search firms for an additional fee of $53. Currently serves over 900 employers, with over 3,000 job seekers in the pool.

MedSearch America, Inc.
15254 NE 95th Street
Redmond, WA 98052
206-883-7252
FAX 206-883-7465
E-mail: office@medsearch.com
gopher.medsearch.com 9001
http://www.medsearch.com:9001

Comprehensive job posting and resume database service for healthcare professionals nationwide. Covers healthcare prositions at all levels. Also has online Healthcareer forums, online healthcare employment articles, industry outlooks and more. No fee for access by job seeker. MedSearch America specializes in candidates in the health care and related fields. This is one of the newer services now available, and does not charge a fee to job seekers. Currently, it serves about 50 employers and has over 400 candidates.

The Monster Board
http://www.monster.com

The Monster Board, run by advertising/recruiting firm ADION Information Services, includes over 500 position listings from more than 70 companies. Most of the jobs are on the east coast (primarily New England) in the computing field, but marketing, communications, and other positions are posted as well. Searching can be done by company name, location, discipline, industry, and specific job title. Resumes can be entered on an on-line form.

HispanData
360 South Hope Avenue
Suite 300c
Santa Barbara, CA 93105
805-682-5843
FAX 805-687-4546

This resume database, created to respond to the need for bilingual capabilities, a diverse work force, and the passage of NAFTA contains 15,000 resumes of Hispanic professionals including new college grads and senior executives. The majority are skilled professionals with 3–5 plus years of work experience in sales, marketing, management, accounting, finance, human resources, systems management/engineering and computer science. Cost is $25 for lifetime enrollment to have resume online. Hispan-Data is slated to be on the Internet by the end of '95.

RESOURCES FOR ANSWERING COMMONLY ASKED QUESTIONS

The following are the kinds of questions often asked by graduates seeking their first career positions. Each question is grouped with a list of suggested sources where the answers may be found. The questions fall into five categories:

1. Location

2. Industries

3. Companies

4. Employment Organizations

5. Generic (Crossover)

QUESTIONS	SOURCE FOR ANSWERS

1. LOCATION

What companies are nearby?

- State industrial directories
- *Dun & Bradstreet Reference Book of Corporate Management*
- Regional development agencies
- State and local Chambers of Commerce
- Telephone directories
- Business sections of local newspapers

In what state(s) does a company have facilities?

- Moody's manuals
- *Directory of Corporate Affiliations*
- Company 10Ks and annual reports
- *Job Seeker's Guide to Private and Public Companies*

2. INDUSTRIES

What are the high-growth industries today?

- Value Line Investment Surveys
- Predicasts forecast manuals
- Refer to *Directory of Industry Data Sources* for other sources

What are the salary levels in specific industries?

- American Compensation Association publications
- *The American Almanac of Jobs and Salaries*
- American Management Association surveys

	• National Association of Colleges and Employers (formerly College Placement Council) salary survey
Who are a firm's competitors?	• *Dun & Bradstreet Million Dollar Directory* (list of other companies making the same product) • *Standard & Poor's Industry Survey* • Business periodicals index • Industry Buying Guides
What industries use specific types of individuals?	• *Encyclopedia of Associations* • National Trade and Professional Associations of the United States (identify appropriate organizations, obtain membership lists, note companies and industries) • *Directory of U.S. Labor Organizations* (identify associations, obtain names of elected officials and department heads) • *Job Seeker's Guide to Private and Public Companies* • Check your library for other occupational guidebooks

3. COMPANIES

| How can I identify the products a company makes? | • Company annual report
• Moody's manuals |

- *Thomas Register* (company catalog volumes)
- *U.S. Industrial Directory*
- American Business Disc (CD-ROM)
- Company Profile (CD-ROM)

What companies make certain products?

- *Thomas Register* (product volumes)
- *Dun & Bradstreet Million Dollar Directory*
- *Standard & Poor's Register of Corporations, Directors, and Executives*
- *Standard Directory of Advertisers*
- *Dun's Electronic Business Directory*

How can I identify consulting organizations by their field?

- *Consultants and Consulting Organizations Directory* (and companion directories)
- There are also many industry-specific directories of consultants; see the *Directory of Directories*

What are sources of company reports and analyses?

- Standard & Poor's Stock Report
- Moody's Investors Fact Sheets
- Value Line Investment Surveys
- Disclosure Database (CD-ROM)
- Some libraries may subscribe to other stock analysis services

What are management's
practices concerning
training?

- Company annual reports
  (employee relations sec-
  tion)
- Membership directories for
  training organizations (e.g.
  American Society for Train-
  ing and Development)
- *The Career Guide—Dun's
  Employment Opportunities
  Directory*
- Peterson's guides

Who are the key people in
the company and what are
their backgrounds?

- *Dun & Bradstreet Reference
  Book of Corporate Manage-
  ment*
- *Standard & Poor's Register
  of Corporations, Directors,
  and Executives*
- *Who's Who* directories
- Corporate proxy statements

Who are the people in
various lines of business?

- *Dun & Bradstreet American
  Corporate Families*
- State industrial directories
- Company annual reports
- Other directories (refer to
  the *Directory of Directories*
  and *Directory of Industry
  Data Sources* for direction)

4. Employment Organizations

What are the names of em-
ployment agencies and/or
executive search firms?

- *The Directory of Executive
  Recruiters*
- *Job Hunters' Sourcebook*
- Directories produced by
  state or local associations

How do I find out about government employment opportunities?

- State: The State Administrative Officials Classified by Functions has a section listing state employment offices and their phone numbers.
- Federal: The U.S. Office of Personnel Management (1900 E Street NW, Washington, DC) is responsible for nationwide recruiting for Civil Service positions at GS levels 1-15. This office also maintains a network of federal job information centers in major metropolitan areas. Phone numbers are listed in local telephone books under U.S. Government, Office of Personnel Management.

5. GENERIC

There may be questions that surface that are not contained in the above categories.

- The Wall Street Journal Index (CD-ROM)
- Business Index—Public Edition
- ABI/Inform Ondisc

As you can see, there is a lot of information available to you and a lot of places you can explore. The key to a successful job search process is to leave no stone unturned. It really is up to you.

CHAPTER 6

Job Search Strategies and Skills

As you explore various industries and organizations through the sources cited in the preceding chapter, you may well develop information that either confirms an earlier interest in a particular career or presents information about an industry and selected companies that pique your interest for the first time. Either will give you a general direction in which to begin moving—perhaps investigating several fields that are of interest to you. Your next step is to gain more insight into what the work is really like—the kinds of people you may be working with, the cultures of companies who employ people in these careers, and some of the issues facing those companies and their people today.

NETWORKING

Your job search needs to be a proactive endeavor, not a reactive one. You need to be in control of what happens. An interesting statistic that needs to be recognized is that 70 to 80 percent of all jobs are never advertised. What this means is that your major job search focus should be on developing your network. So let's look at the concept of a network and networking.

What Is a Network?

The term network is both a noun and a verb. As a noun, a *network* is defined as a group of individuals who are connected to and cooperate with each other. As a verb, to *network* is to develop contacts and exchange information with other people for purposes of developing business or expanding one's career. The verb form often becomes action-oriented and is changed to *networking*.

Learning how to develop your network is one of the most important skills for managing your career. A network often looks like a spider's web because it is interconnected and goes out in many directions.

One of the first questions that is asked and needs to be answered is "Who belongs on my network list?" There are few exclusions, so virtually anyone you know would be a good candidate. Let's take a few moments to begin the creation of your network. Either by yourself or with one or more friends, brainstorm a list of the types of people you know, for example, doctors, lawyers, accountants, barbers/ hairdressers, relatives, etc. Remember, there are no limitations to who can be part of your network. Next, start adding the names of specific people you know in these categories. Develop your network in the space below. Start with your name in the middle and then work outward.

YOUR NETWORK

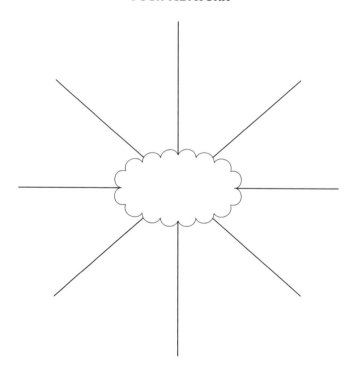

Add more lines, moving to other sheets as your network expands. You can probably put 25 people in your network with relative ease. Would you agree that each of those people probably knows at least 25 other people? Your network has now expanded to 625 people and they each probably know another 25 people, who know 25 more people, and so on. As you can see, it doesn't take very long for your network to grow. It has been said that anyone is only three or four contacts away from meeting nearly anyone he or she wants to meet. Don't forget that your teachers and fellow students are also part of your network.

Your network is developing every day. Explore areas that you may not have thought about, such as the local Chamber of Commerce. What is the cost of becoming a member and participating in its activities? Do you subscribe to professional and business journals? Many of them have student rates with deep discounts. Is there an alumni organization at your school? Have you given any thought to contacting members who are in the field in which you have an interest? Why not? Your network does not develop without effort on your part.

Your network will be your primary source for contacts for informational interviews. This topic is covered in much greater detail in the chapter on interviews.

Your personal network is a powerful tool that can help put you in touch with people who can give you good, solid information about your potential career field—through the informational interview—and people who can also put you in touch with still other people who can help you in your job search.

USING PRIVATE EMPLOYMENT AGENCIES

Employment agencies can be a useful part of your job search, but it's important to understand how they work, how they can help you, and how to use them to your own best advantage. The section that follows concerns only private employment agencies, not executive search firms, which usually work for client companies rather than individuals. In addition, the executive search firms typically are looking for more senior-level managers and other very experienced employees.

There are two types of agencies—permanent and temporary. Sometimes they are two divisions of the same firm. And you may consider registering with both of them. "Temping" can give you some income while you continue your search for a regular position, and the experience will give you a good inside look at a number of companies. Also, you may receive an offer of regular employment if a company likes what you do for them as a temp. As one corporate recruiter states, "We end up hiring about 35 percent of the people who come in as temporary employees into regular positions." If the job search is not as productive as you were hoping, consider signing up with a temporary agency.

Most employment agencies concentrate their efforts on entry-level, technical, and first-line supervisory positions. They frequently avoid working with job seekers with no experience because their clients may not be interested in paying a fee for an inexperienced candidate. If you truly have little or no work experience, it may not make sense to invest your time and energy pursuing various employment agencies.

If you do choose to contact an employment agency, do not turn your job search over to this or any other third party, as they are primarily loyal to their agency and collecting the fees for placing people. Use them only as a supplement to your own activities. Experts in the employment field recommend that you devote no more than about ten percent of your search time to working with an agency.

It is estimated that there are probably eight to ten thousand private employment agencies in the U.S. today. Many agencies specialize in certain industries—banking, accounting, data processing, medical services, or engineering, for example—and often prefer to work only with experienced applicants. Other agencies place clerical workers and secretaries. But some agencies do specialize in working with recent college graduates. Most are listed in the telephone book. A phone call will determine if it is the right agency for your needs. Many of the agencies that work with recent college graduates will develop relationships with campus career centers, so check with your center for any recommendations.

Here are some insights into how agencies work and how you can work with one to your own best advantage:

Nearly all sizable companies work with employment agencies; many become closely allied with one or two agencies and give them most of their business.

Agencies are not usually "retained" by an employer—they work on a contingency basis. If they don't fill a job opening, they don't get paid. There was an individual who was sent on a job interview by an agency. When he arrived for the interview at 1:00 P.M. he was told that the manager was tied up in a meeting. Three and a half hours later, he met with the manager only to find out that no interview had been arranged and no agreement existed between the agency and the company. The agency was hoping to earn a commission in any way it could. This is uncommon, but it can happen.

Most agencies today also work on a "fee paid" basis—meaning the employer pays their fee for filling a job. Whenever possible, you should lean toward this type of arrangement. Otherwise, it could get to be very expensive for you.

However, some agencies still look to the job seeker for their commission—a hefty percentage of the person's first year's salary. Were you to contract with such an agency, it might legally require you to pay its fee even if you quit the new job a few weeks after taking it. Some agencies have a dual fee arrangement—the individual pays part of the fee and the employer pays part of the fee.

If an agency asks you to sign any form, read it very carefully. It may be a contract requiring you to pay for its services. If you agree to do this, ask how long you must keep a job before you are obligated to pay the fee—and get an answer in writing.

Do not sign an agreement to work with any agency exclusively. Some job seekers who do, wind up paying the agency for a job they got for themselves. Again, read any agreements carefully, and don't sign anything that you don't understand or that has questionable language.

"Plan your work for today and every day, then work your plan."
—Norman Vincent Peale

Remember, an employer who hires you through an agency is likely paying more for your services than had you been hired on the open market. This means that the agency may be getting some of your first year's income whether or not you pay it directly.

Insist that any agency check with you before sending your resume to any prospective employer; you don't want it duplicating your own efforts. In addition, there may be some companies in which you have no interest. Agencies can work against you by calling firms you've already contacted and trying to place other candidates they represent. So be wary about saying too much about your own job search.

Ask people in your network to recommend agencies with which they've had a good experience. When you get a firm's name, ask your contact for the name of the recruiter with whom he or she worked.

It's best to make your initial contact with an agency in person. After setting up an interview with a particular recruiter by phone, go there. While he or she is interviewing you, you can also interview the recruiter. Find out how long the person has been with the agency and in the agency field. Check out the offices and find out about their standards. Is it a quality operation? Are these the kind of people you feel you can work with comfortably? Do you believe they will represent you well? How much pressure do you feel in the initial interview? If they're pressuring you, chances are they're doing the same thing with employers.

John Kniering, from the University of Hartford Career Center, recalls an incident when he worked in the human resources department of a corporation. "An agency we had worked with sent us a group of resumes for a software engineering position. Included in the stack of resumes was one from one of our own employees. I went down to see the individual. He apologized and told me he had no idea the agency would do something like that. He severed his relationship with that agency the same day."

Mr. Kniering indicates that most students have not had

good luck with agencies. "The ones who had good experiences were typically referred to a specific individual within an agency by a friend, acquaintance, or fellow student who had a positive experience."

Remember, you are free to say "no" to an interview or a job offer. And if you don't like the way the agency is handling their part of your search, you can decide not to work with them further.

Employment agencies do know where current openings are, and they can get you interviews. However, even if you're working with an agency, you should not abdicate to them or any other entity your responsibility for finding a position.

"Paralyze resistance with persistence."
—WOODY HAYES

If you do decide to work with an agency, check with it regularly. It can give you feedback from interviews it arranges. And, through regular contact, you can determine what it's doing in your behalf. Don't forget, it is your job search! And you may find it necessary to be assertive with the agency to maintain control of that search and to use the agency to your own best advantage.

NEWSPAPER ADS

Big city newspapers often have pages of ads for job openings. Smalltown papers will have fewer ads, but they should be checked regularly. In most areas, the Sunday paper is the focus of employers. If you are going to relocate and want the ads from a paper in that area, most will be happy to mail you copies of the paper. Make sure that you pay for first-class postage. It may cost more, but it will arrive within a few days rather than three to four weeks. Remember, responding to ads is a reactive process not a proactive one.

Other job sources include:

- Business newspapers
- School/university job postings
- Association newsletters
- Bulletin boards in community centers
- Trade publications
- Government publications
- On-line services

Keep in mind that in many cases, fewer than ten percent of the local jobs available at any given time are ever listed in the local newspaper or many of the other sources listed above. So use the newspaper and these other sources, but don't rely on them too heavily. They should never be your sole—or even major—source for employment leads.

Job advertisements are valuable for another reason as well. You can use them as a tool for assessing the labor market, especially if you are trying to choose between a couple of distant locations. For example, if over a period of a few months you see that there seems to be five times as many advertisements in the newspaper for city A than for city B, that should indicate to you that your efforts will be much more productive if you focus on city A.

Two Types of Job Ads

Open ads list the company's name, usually with address and phone number and a name to contact. After responding to these ads, you can follow up by phone to determine whether your letter and resume were received . . . and possibly even get the employer's reaction to them.

Blind ads are "lower yield" than open ads. They don't reveal the company name, and the reply address will often be a post office box number or a box at the local newspaper. Companies publish blind ads for several reasons. The company doesn't want to respond to every candidate; that takes time and money. And it doesn't want to be inundated by job seekers following up on their applications by phone. It may also not want the public or present employees to know that some key personnel change is about to occur. If the ad lists a post office box, you can go to the post office and ask who has taken out the box. The newspaper will not divulge this information.

"Success is never final, and failure is never fatal."

—ANONYMOUS

In some cases, there may not be a job opening at all. The ad may have been placed by an employment agency seeking to stockpile resumes to use when the next real opening does occur. In at least one instance, an employer placed a blind ad in the newspaper when no job existed. The senior manager was interested in finding out how many current employees would respond to the ad. He was checking for company loyalty. You may not see this as very ethical, but it can happen, so exercise caution. If you are currently employed and your employer does not know that you are looking for another position, use caution when responding to a blind ad. In addition to the reason stated above, you don't know who will receive your resume and whom your manager may know.

Which ads should you respond to? Even if you don't have all the qualifications for a position that interests you, respond anyway. Ads often describe the "ideal candidate," which companies rarely find. Also, look for companies that run large ads listing many openings. Even if your qualifications aren't exactly right for a listed position, there may be other current or future openings for which you would be an excellent candidate.

How to answer an ad? Those that include a phone number may expect a call, but not always. In some cases the phone number is listed to enable potential applicants to ask questions. In many cases, it will be an employment agency. If you have the choice between calling and writing, call. You'll have the opportunity to establish some rapport over the phone and learn more precisely the qualifications that are desired by the interviewer. In some cases, companies include a fax number and ask that candidates fax their resumes. In any event, if there is no name listed but the company is identified, call to get the name of the appropriate person to whom the resume and cover letter should be addressed. This will also give you a name for follow-up contact.

When you call, have your notes handy, which outline your strengths as they apply to that position. This will help you speak quickly and clearly about yourself. And don't be hesitant to ask questions—your concerns are important. You don't want to waste your time interviewing for a position that doesn't really suit you.

Blind ads, of course, require a written response. But even some that list a company's name may only receive applications by mail. However, if you do know the company's name, some of your contacts may be able to help you "network" your way into the firm for an interview.

Some Tips for Responding to an Ad

Before writing a letter or making a phone call, you need to do your homework.

Identify the key assets or traits the advertiser seems to be seeking. Write them out and underline key words.

List your own assets, experience, or traits that match those in the ad.

Try to work these into a "double table" of needs and assets. This can become a critical part of your phone response—or a key to your written follow-up.

If you're writing, make the rest of your letter short and sweet. If it's appropriate, you can refer to your attached resume.

Try to avoid the issue of salary requirements, reserving this, it is to be hoped, for an interview.

One last thing: send your letter out three or four days after the ad is published. There will be less competition, and perhaps the recruiter will be able to spend a little more time reading your resume.

Here are two sample letters for following up on a newspaper ad. The first is a response to an "open" ad:

Michael Dillon
103 East 90th Street
New York, NY 10028
212–555–1898

June 21, 1995

Mr. William Johnson
Manufacturing Manager
DONCO Products, Inc.
123 Main Street
White Plains, NY 13480

Dear Mr. Johnson:

Please accept the enclosed resume in response to your advertisement in the June 18, 1995, edition of the *New York Times* for a Marketing Trainee at DONCO Products. I believe my strong background in direct selling may be of great value to you.

While working on my bachelor's degree in business at NYU, I spent two summers doing a variety of line production work and two other summers selling consumer products in a retail outlet. In addition, I often acted as an assistant store manager in times of peak sales volumes, especially during holiday periods.

I have been successful in several areas I think will be of interest to a growing firm like DONCO Products. In particular, I have:

- Increased sales significantly for a long-term obsolescent product; and,
- Assisted in motivating a part-time sales staff during busy holiday periods.

Thank you for your consideration. I will contact you on Thursday, July 6, to respond to any questions you may have. I look forward to speaking with you soon. You may reach me by mail at the above address, or by phone.

Sincerely,
Michael Dillon

Enclosure

And, this is a typical response to a "blind" ad:

Dorothy Conlin
61 Perry Street
New York, NY 10014
(212) 555-2121

June 21, 1995

Box F5861
The *New York Times*
New York, NY 10108

To Whom It May Concern:

I have enclosed my resume in response to your advertisement in the June 18, 1995, edition of the *New York Times* for a Customer Service Administrator.

For the past two years I have been employed part-time in the Customer Service Department of the D-J Textile Company while completing my degree in marketing at City College. My duties at D-J Textile include working at a CRT terminal, taking over-the-phone purchase orders, and responding to customer complaints—making adjustments to their accounts as necessary.

Thank you for your time and consideration. I look forward to receiving your reply in the near future.

Sincerely,
Dorothy Conlin

Enclosure

Networking, informational interviewing, perhaps using employment agencies, and responding to ads in newspapers and other publications are all useful strategies in a thorough, well-organized, and successful job search. Alone, not one of them is sufficient. However, used together—even synergistically—they can help move you from student to interviewee and potential employee. To move beyond this point, you'll need to do just a bit more "homework"—perfecting your resume, cover letters, and both interviewing and negotiating skills for your first career position after college.

SEARCH TIP

A job search is not the time to "wing" your performance. You must be thoroughly prepared with knowledge and homework prior to any interview.

According to Jackie Larson in the "Manager's Journal" in the April 17, 1995, issue of *The Wall Street Journal*, "Those candidates who got the offers knew their biggest challenge was to get and keep their resumes in front of a potential hiring manager. They weren't afraid to use the telephone, even though it was necessary to continually 'cold call' people with whom they had no personal relationship. By making those calls, these candidates located jobs that weren't known to the general public—in a few cases, they even created the openings themselves." He goes on to say, "Few job hunters make this kind of effort. But for those who do, it pays off."

In many cases, the initial inquiry results in a "We don't

have any openings." According to Mr. Larson, "It is important to persist after an initial objection. I'm always amazed at how afraid people are to continue a conversation after I say, 'I don't have any openings in that area.' Successful candidates don't take no for an answer. They ask what my time frames and future hiring plans might be, and they ask if they can keep in touch with me on a regular basis. They also ask for names of other managers in other departments or even other companies that are doing well. They network for additional leads and ask if they can use my name as an introductory reference."

SEARCH TIP

Don't let yourself fall into any passive or waiting-game scenarios. Wherever possible, be the person who follows up with a contact or lead, and the one who calls a potential employer to see if an interview can be arranged.

If you get an interview, you may not get the job. But, if you don't get an interview, you will never be considered for the job. That is the *key*, getting the interview.

CHAPTER 7

Making Contact:

Letters and Correspondence

Nearly as important as the resume you prepare and the interview you give is the quality of the correspondence you send out. In many cases, it is your first contact with a prospective employer and the first impression that the organization has of you. There are two major types of correspondence that you will prepare—the cover letter to accompany your resume and the thank you to extend your appreciation for being considered for an opportunity.

SEARCH TIP

Understand that you and your aspirations are not going to be a priority to any business person no matter what you may have to offer. Ignore indifference; go forward with energy, enthusiasm, and persistence to get where you want to go.

COVER LETTERS

By definition, cover letters are brief communications that accompany your resume when you mail it. What you write in your letter depends on the reason you're sending your resume.

A Good Cover Letter

Uses a standard business format and employs a business or professional tone.

Is written to an individual, if possible, not to a function or to "Dear Sir or Madam." If the name is not listed, call the company and ask who is receiving resumes for that position. If you are unable to determine an appropriate person, address your letter "To Whom It May Concern."

Is written on the same paper stock (and color) as your resume.

Is just as neat, visually attractive, and error-free as your resume.

Includes your home telephone number and your work or office number, if it is permissible to receive calls there.

Is three to five paragraphs in length—written on a single page.

Tells the recipient why you are writing (response to an ad, referral by a mutual friend, etc.).

Specifies the position (or type of position) you are interested in filling.

Speaks to the needs and interests of the reader; demonstrates that your education, abilities, and interests are relevant to his or her job opening.

Lets the reader know that you know something about his or her company, that you've gone to the trouble of doing some research before writing.

States your key skills and abilities.

Should always be individually typed or written on a word processor with a letter quality printer; *never* send a photocopy of a generic cover letter.

Has a conversational tone but does not presume a friendship with the reader.

States how you would like the recipient to respond or states that you will follow up by telephone on a specified date or during a certain week. The preference is for you to be proactive in the process.

Requests an interview.

Thanks the reader.

Closes with *Sincerely* or *Yours truly*—*Cordially* may seem presumptuous.

The last line in the letter should be the word *Enclosure*, because your resume is enclosed with the letter.

A couple of sample cover letters follow.

Sample Cover Letter A

Margaret Greenacre
1001 Long Street
Marietta, GA 30068
(404) 555–3882

[Date]

Ms. Marion W. Crane
Vice-President
First National Bank
100 Main Street
Knoxville, TN 37902

Dear Ms. Crane:

A friend of my parents, Joan Cooper in your Commercial Lending Department, recently told me the bank may be seeking a marketing assistant. As you can see from my resume, I am about to complete my BS degree in business administration with a concentration in marketing at Georgia State University. I have attended GSU in the evenings while working full time at Trust Company Bank in Atlanta.

Some of my present responsibilities include:

- Overseeing the services provided by an outside public relations firm.
- Coordinating the gathering of demographic data on present customers.
- Supervising a staff of clerical assistants.

Thank you for your time and consideration. I would very much like to meet with you to discuss your open position. I will phone you next Tuesday, the 12th, in the afternoon to ask if I might meet with you for an interview. Should you want to reach me before then, please phone me at home at (404) 555-3882.

Sincerely,
Margaret Greenacre

Enclosure

Sample Cover Letter B

Diana Browning
92 West Davis Street
Pittsburgh, PA 32618
412–555–9070

[Date]

Dr. William L. Green
Director, Medical Testing Department
L. L. Magers Medical Center
122 Evergreen Drive
Bethlehem, PA 18515

Dear Dr. Green:

I am writing in response to your ad in the *Pittsburgh Dispatch* on [day and date] for a Coordinator of Medical Assistants. As you requested, I am enclosing a resume summarizing my education, qualifications, and work experience.

In line with your advertisement, my summer and part-time work experience includes:

- Exercise testing
- Blood pressure monitoring
- Coordinating activities of medical assistants

I am graduating from the University of Pittsburgh in May and plan to move to the Lehigh Valley area around the first of July. I would like very much to meet you to discuss employment opportunities with your medical center. I will be in touch with your office by phone next week to arrange for a meeting or to answer any questions you might have. However, if you should want to reach me before that time, please phone me at (412) 555-9070.

Thank you for your time and consideration.

Sincerely,
Diana Browning

Enclosure

THE FOLLOW-UP OR THANK-YOU LETTER

Within 48 hours after an interview, it's good form to send a cordial follow-up or thank-you letter to the person with whom you spoke. If you interviewed with more than one person, an original note should be sent to each person. It is amazing how many people still don't do this. This letter should:

Thank the person for the interview.

Emphasize your interest in the position under consideration.

Re-phrase your background and briefly explain how your experience can complement the requirements of the position.

Identify two or three things of interest that came up in the interview.

State anything you wish you had made clearer—or forgot to mention—in the interview.

Indicate that you look forward to hearing his or her decision (refer to the follow-up agreed to) or say that you will follow up to determine when the interviewer wants to see you again.

"Politeness costs nothing and gains everything."

—ANONYMOUS

Another way of recalling the construction of this follow-up letter is *The 4 Rs*:

Remember—Since most people don't take the time to send follow-up letters, yours will stand out and help the interviewer remember you.

Reinforce—In a sentence or two, restate the skills, accomplishments, and experience that make you right for this job.

Recoup—If there's something you wish you had made clearer—or forgot to say in the interview—you can state it now in your letter.

Remind—In the closing paragraph, you can tactfully remind the interviewer of a promise or agreement. ("Thank you for your interest and encouragement. I look forward to hearing from you by next Wednesday to learn the date of my next interview.")

Sample Follow-up Letter

Barbara J. Gardner
1234 54th Street
New York, NY 10017
212-555-9921

June 24, 1995

Ms. Alice Mann
Employment Director
ABC Hotels, Inc.
123 Main Street
Rochester, NY 11111

Dear Ms. Mann:

(Remember) I appreciated the opportunity to meet with you yesterday to learn more about your organization. It was also thoughtful of you to introduce me to Gail Graf and John Slingerland.

(Reinforce) As we discussed, my education in hotel/motel management at Cornell and my three years' experience with Hyatt Hotels would indicate a good fit for the position as Banquet Director. The position would make good use of my detail-orientation, planning abilities, and experience in handling major corporate customers.

(Recoup) When we discussed my computer skills, I'm not sure I made it clear that I'll be concluding my training on Lotus 1-2-3 next week. I'm sure this could be helpful during budget reviews.

(Remind) I have a strong interest in the position, and I will phone you next Tuesday as you suggested to discuss the next steps.

Sincerely,
Barbara J. Gardner

SEARCH TIP

Be prepared for communication curve balls in your job search:

- *Do not fax things to potential employers without letting them know in advance, as there is a chance it won't reach the person you sent it to in an environment of many fax machines and multiple users.*

- *Never pick up the phone to speak with a contact or potential employer without knowing exactly what you are going to say. If you call someone and get his or her voice mail, don't get caught by surprise.*

- *People will likely expect you to have an answering machine, and be able to fax them your resume.*

CHAPTER 8

Interviews

Interviews can fall into three categories—the informational interview, the on-campus interview, and the job interview. Let's look at each of them in more detail.

THE INFORMATIONAL INTERVIEW

Your network serves many purposes. One of the ways to gain the insights discussed in the first paragraph is through using your personal network to get informational interviews. An informational interview is just what is says—an interview in which you gain information about an organization, a career field, or a position. Informational interviews differ from actual employment interviews in several ways:

You are there earnestly seeking information, not to sell yourself as a job candidate. Many who are impressive in the interview do get leads for internships and even for jobs.

You can control the focus of the interview by the

questions you ask. Remember, your purpose is to gain information.

This type of interview will likely be easier to arrange than the job interview.

You're not being "graded" by a prospective employer, so you will probably be more at ease.

However, don't let the lack of pressure make you feel so comfortable that you forget either your good manners or your business and professional ethics. You have asked the person across the desk for his or her time and thoughtful answers. Even if you think you see an opening for a real job, don't even hint at it. For one thing, you're really not ready for an employment interview yet; you're still gathering information. For another, the person you're interviewing may feel you got this appointment under false pretenses, and feel justifiably upset or angry or both. In any case, such a response from someone employed in a field that interests you can't do you any good later on. In the event that you are asked if you are interested in being interviewed for a position, schedule it for a different time when both of you will be more prepared.

"Failure is only the opportunity to more intelligently begin again."
— HENRY FORD

How do you locate potential interviewees? Through the personal network you developed above. Though you may not have used it extensively, you do have a network. Some universities have alumni who have agreed to conduct information interviews with current and former students. Check with your placement office. If it does not have one, maybe it will get one started.

Your network consists of two sets of people. One set will be "warm contacts"—people with whom you have some connection. Those you have no connection with are "cold contacts." Warm contacts may also include peers—perhaps a friend who graduated a year or two back who's now working in a career that interests you. Warm contacts can also include the parents of your college friends, and friends and associates of your parents, relatives, and other friends. In short, warm contacts probably know you or know of you.

Before you write the members of this group asking for an interview, you might ask the person you know mutually to inquire informally if the contact would be welcomed. That's a communication that can be handled in person—perhaps over lunch or at a business meeting—or by phone. It really serves to open the door for you. Your first communication with the potential contact should be a brief letter requesting his or her time in a short meeting.

"Cold contacts" are people you don't know. You may get their names from business directories or people who know them. A suggestion is to start as high up in the organization as possible. For example, if you are interested in marketing, your first cold contact could be the VP of Sales and Marketing. He or she may determine that you should speak with a manager or director and refer you to that person. The cold contact becomes somewhat warmer because of the internal referral. Be sure to thank the person for the referral. Because these interviews may not be quite as comfortable as those with your warm contacts, it's probably a good idea to start with the latter.

Your letter requesting the interview should be only three or four paragraphs in length. Begin by telling the individual the purpose of the letter, who you are, where you are in school, when you'll graduate, why you're interested in his or her career field, that you're presently gathering information on that field, and that you'd appreciate twenty to thirty minutes of his or her time to learn more about the career and what it's like to be in it. Make your tone friendly but businesslike. Remember, you're likely asking a busy professional to take time out of the day to do you a favor. You might even want to acknowledge this in the letter itself. Then, close with something like, "I'd like to phone you on [day and date, and specify morning or afternoon] to ask when it might be convenient to meet." The call should follow the letter by no more than ten days. Be available to meet with the person at his or her convenience—early morning, late afternoon, etc.

"The secret of success is constancy of purpose."

—BENJAMIN DISRAELI

Then, be certain to follow up with that phone call on the day you indicated. Business people appreciate consistency and being able to count on people to do what they say they'll do. When you speak to your contact, make it clear that you definitely want only twenty to thirty minutes of his or her time. When the appointment is confirmed, repeat the day, date, and time—"Fine, that's Thursday the eighth, at 9:30 A.M. I look forward to seeing you then."

Before you go on the interview, though, make sure you do some more "homework." There is a lot of information you can get about a person's business and his or her career from sources mentioned in the previous chapter. Don't take his or her time asking questions you could (and should) have answered before your meeting. Your preparation will be appreciated, and you'll be much more comfortable in the interview.

After you've done your research, make a list of questions you either could not answer through other material, or, perhaps, information you'd like your contact to confirm or expand on. Actually write out your questions and prioritize them. You want to make sure that you get the answers to your most important questions because you only have twenty to thirty minutes. And consider leaving room between the questions to note your answers during the interview.

Thought-Starters:

What interested you in this career? Why do you believe it's a good career choice?

If you were choosing a career today, would you make the same choice? Why or why not?

What is most satisfying about your career? Do you enjoy coming to work every day?

If your son or daughter wanted to follow in your footsteps, what would you tell him or her?

What are the most important qualifications to succeed in this job?

What is your typical day like?

What do you like most about this field? What do you like least?

What was your biggest success? Your biggest disappointment?

What are the big issues in your field today?

What are the major problems? Opportunities?

How has your field changed since you entered it?

How secure is this field today? Is it growing or shrinking?

How rapidly can someone expect to advance in this career?

What can one expect to be doing and earning in two years? In five?

How much competition is there among your peers?

If you could give me one solid piece of advice, what would it be?

Is there anything else I should have asked but didn't?

Before you conclude the conversation, be sure to ask if your contact can suggest other people with whom you should talk. You'll be expanding your personal network geometrically, and people who are active and successful in a career are the best source for introductions to other people like them. Make sure that you are ready to leave at the end of your agreed-upon time. The only exception is if the individual asks you to stay longer. But make sure that you are not imposing.

If your interview goes well and your contact doesn't

seem to be in a hurry to end it, consider asking if you might have a brief tour of the office or work area. In many cases, your contact may extend this offer, perhaps even in the middle of the interview. This will give you the opportunity to pick up some notion of what it's actually like to work in this field. You'll also gain some valuable first-hand impressions of actual businesses that employ people in that career. This may be very helpful later on when you're deciding whom to approach for an employment interview. Remember the 80–20 rule: you should be doing only 20 percent of the talking in the information interview. In the job interview, you should be doing 80 percent.

"Be grateful for luck, but don't depend on it."
—ANONYMOUS

After each interview, be sure to write your contact a note of appreciation for his or her time and thoughtful answers. This thank-you note should be sent within 48 hours. It can be handwritten, if you have good penmanship, or typed. If a friend or relative helped set up the contact, a note or phone call confirming that you have had the interview is also appropriate.

Don't stop with one or two informational interviews in each field that interests you. By talking with a number of people, you will see some trends emerging—and you will be closer still to making your decision based on solid information and the "vibes" you get from those you interview.

Write a brief summary of the experience after each interview. A 5 x 7 card is a good place to make these notes. You can file them for later reference when you want to recall how a place "felt" and the impressions you gained while you were there. Cross-referencing these cards with your notes from the interview is a good idea, too. If you use a computer and have one of the numerous "client tracking" software programs available, you may keep track of the information this way.

SEARCH TIP

Modesty and restraint are respectable traits, but in a job search self-promotion and aggressive initiative rule the day. These are the norms that everyone expects.

In summary, the informational interview is an excellent fact-finding strategy. It puts you face-to-face with people who are making a career in a field that interests you. You'll gain valuable insights into how these people react to their world of work . . . and how that world is treating them. You may not care for all the people you interview. Some you may take to instantly and even strike up a friendship. But if you come up against a full dozen people in the same field who are cranky and dissatisfied with their lot in life, you will have received a strong message that it might make sense to shift gears and consider another field. On the other hand, one or two of those you interview for informational purposes could even become your mentors.

THE ON-CAMPUS INTERVIEW

These interviews differ from those conducted in a company's offices in several important ways:

Since most campus interviews last only thirty minutes, there is significant time pressure on the interviewer.

The company office interview centers around the question, "To hire or not to hire?" The campus interview is much more of an information-gathering exercise in which the interviewer's principal responsibility is to identify and quantify the most attractive job candidates.

Because he or she may already have interviewed a number of candidates, the interviewer may not be well focused on your discussion; fatigue and boredom can be a problem for both of you.

Unlike the company office interview, the interviewer knows he or she must also "sell" the company to interviewees.

The Campus Interview Model

A model for the campus interview has been constructed by industry to minimize the impact of the three realities listed above: time pressure, fatigue and boredom, and the need to sell. This model has been widely used by a number of major corporations and has been found to work well in most on-campus situations. Knowing the other side's strategy is always a major factor in winning. If he or she is following the widely accepted model, the interviewer's strategy looks like this:

1. Opening comments

2. Specific facts

3. Broad-brush questions

4. Applicant's job wants

5. Sell the company

6. Applicant's questions

7. Next steps

Here is a point-for-point analysis of this interview model, using our knowledge of the constraints, demands, and pressures on the interviewer to provide insights that should prove helpful to you in this interview situation.

Opening comments

Because time is at a premium, the interviewer will likely devote only three to five minutes to establishing rapport with you. And you may find, to your absolute delight, that you are more at ease than your interviewer. After all, this is your turf! The interviewer will, of course, feel the need to control the situation. However, he or she realizes he or she cannot dominate the discussion. He or she also wants to hear from you and learn more about the type of person you are and the things that are important to you in a career position. During these opening moments, you may hear your interviewer say something like:

"I know that in our meeting today we are both attempting to learn a little about what we can offer each other. I certainly would like to learn about your background and interests. And I know you are interested in learning about what our company has to offer. So let's divide up the time a bit. I'd like to spend the first half of the interview getting acquainted with you, then we'll turn it around and you can learn more about us. Okay?"

Specific facts

Most organizations that conduct campus interviews insist that their representatives gather certain specific information about job candidates. To avoid running out of time and failing to get this data by waiting until near the end of the interview, you can expect to be asked, early on, at least four things:

To sign a transcript request for the release of your academic records.

If the address and phone number on your resume are correct and current.

If you expect to graduate in May (or at the end of the present quarter or semester).

If you have had contact with other personnel of the company the interviewer represents.

Some companies send several interviewers to the same campus on the same day. They don't want to duplicate their associates' efforts, nor do they want to have their people sending you multiples of the same interview follow-up letter. (If several different divisions of the same firm are on campus, there is also the issue of your receiving invitations for further interviews from one group and turn-downs from others.)

Broad-brush questions

These are basically open-ended questions designed to make you think "on your feet." By doing this, the interviewer seeks to make certain observations about your behavior, how you think, your poise, and your general personal characteristics. You'll probably get two or three broad-brush questions such as:

"What long-term satisfaction do you expect to derive from a career in _____?"

"How do you evaluate your college career as preparation for the future?"

"What are your thoughts about how (accounting, writing, etc.) will sustain your interest and motivation in the years ahead?"

In listening to you, you may find that the interviewer is accepting the applicant (you) through comments that encourage you to speak out and elaborate—"Uh-huh," "Go on," "I understand," and "That's interesting." Interviewers are taught that such comments encourage conversation without either condemning or condoning what is being said.

You'll also likely hear your interviewer restate and reflect your words. He or she listens, then "mirrors" what you said through other words. The theory is that people will reveal even more information about themselves when they feel accepted and understood.

Be alert for a pause or silence in the interviewer's part of the dialogue. This is said to be one of the most powerful tools in an interviewer's repertoire. When a pause occurs during a discussion, there is tremendous psychological pressure to fill the conversational void. And most of the pressure will be on you, not the interviewer. He or she may intentionally create a silence just to see whether you jump to fill it . . . and, if you do, what you fill it with. If you are the one who pauses, let it be clear that you do so because you're thinking. But again, don't be so eager to end the silence that you wind up saying something you may later regret. This may be a key point to a successful interview.

Applicant's job wants and selling the company

This part of your discussion often combines steps 4 and 5 of the interview model. By finding out what's important to you in a job, the savvy interviewer will also know how best to "sell" the company to you. Your best strategy at this juncture is to be honest in relating what really is important to you in an anticipated employment situation, then listen carefully to whether—and how—your interviewer matches your concerns with either realities or promises about his or her firm.

Applicant's questions

After proceeding through steps 4 and 5, the interviewer will want to entertain any questions you may have. The very nature of those questions will provide definite clues for him or her to assess your desires, motivations, and additional avenues that might successfully sell you on the company. It is important that you have given some thought and taken some time to prepare at least three to five questions for the interviewer. The questions should focus on the organization or department that interests you, growth opportunities, future direction of the company, etc. You will only have a few minutes, so make them count.

SEARCH TIP

Don't feel that only you can speak about you. Pursue your references for recommendations; it will make your search immeasurably easier to have a professor introduce you, or a well-connected friend open doors.

Interviewers are encouraged to be frank and honest in responding to your questions. If you ask something to which he or she has no answer, the response should be, "I don't know, but I'll find out for you." Hearing this is a good indication that the interviewer is "shooting straight" with you on other important points.

Next steps

In many cases, campus interviewers will indicate that you should hear something from the company in about two weeks. However, you shouldn't expect the interviewer to indicate what that communication will be. Interviewers don't want to commit their companies to additional interviews or company visits until they have had the opportunity to review their notes on all interviewees. If you aren't issued an invitation here, don't be discouraged. It may be just too early for one.

Now that you've had a look at the campus interview from the perspective of the other side of the table, perhaps you'll be more relaxed and better able to enjoy these experiences. Take advantage of the opportunity to experience four or five of these interviews. It will help you develop your interviewing skills and get you to thinking about your career in a more tangible way.

Good luck!

THE JOB INTERVIEW

A Perspective on the Interview

Some people believe the job interview is the only way to get a job. However, as you know by now, the interview is actually only a part of the effort. While it is usually an essential element in the search for a position, it is really only the culmination of a lot of other activities.

If you think like a marketer, the job interview is an important selling event that follows a lot of hard work in market research, strategic planning, marketing communications, and other elements of your marketing campaign. The interview is your final marketing event—the last hurdle between you and a job offer. As such, it is well worth your time to prepare for this occasion.

Rarely is someone ever hired for a position (other than perhaps some minimum-wage positions) after only one interview. Typically, there are two or more interview visits with multiple people involved in the interview process. The first visit is typically a screening meeting, often with only the human resources professional who is functioning as the recruiter in this process. This person's job is to qualify you for the next step—meeting with the interview team or the hiring manager. You may look good on paper, but there is more to getting a job than the resume image you have provided. The second and subsequent visits will include meetings with the hiring manager, peers and co-workers, perhaps some people who report to this position, and maybe the hiring manager's boss. Others outside of the department who have good interviewing and assessment skills may also be brought in for their opinions and insights.

As you approach the interview, it is important to keep this reality in mind—the interview is a two-way street. Not only are you being interviewed by the company, you should be interviewing it to see if you want to work for this organization and these individuals. It is an important decision and not one that should be made in haste just because you need a job. Building strong interview skills can help you through a successful job search and into a new job as well. Also, keep in mind the fact that it may take interviews with four or five or more companies before a job offer is extended to you. Don't get discouraged; learn from the experience.

This chapter will help you prepare for your interviews in many ways—from conducting company research and dressing for the occasion to communicating confidence during the interview itself. Your self-confidence is essential to a successful interview. And all the following information is geared to helping you build confidence in yourself and your ability to perform well in the interview situation.

Types of Job Interviews

There are two types of job interviews: the screening interview and the decision interview. Each type is conducted by a different kind of interviewer, and for a different purpose.

Screening interviews

Screening interviews are usually conducted by two groups of people. The *external source* will be representatives from employment agencies and executive search firms. These individuals:

typically are very experienced interviewers (unless they were recently hired);

are working for the client and being paid a commission so they want to *fill the job* as quickly as possible;

are not as concerned with your wants and needs as much as with the clients' wants and needs;

may be able to give you advice and suggestions on your resume and interview style that you may or may not want to take.

The *internal source* will be the human resources professionals who:

typically are also well-trained interviewers;

have been working for the organization for quite a while and therefore know and understand the company and the hiring manager better than the external sources;

have a general idea and understanding of the position for which you are interviewing but who probably don't know all the specifics or understand the technical aspects of the position.

Screening interviewers often work from a general job description supplied by the hiring manager, who may want to see only a few (three or four) applicants. Before sending you on to the hiring manager, the interviewer needs enough information about you to decide whether there is a reasonable match between you and the job. This person is also looking for reasons to screen you out, to eliminate you from further consideration for that position. So be brief, maintain a positive attitude, and don't volunteer information that could eliminate your candidacy. Negative or superfluous information can make it difficult or impossible to get beyond the screening interview. However, a good screening interview, even if you are screened out of this job, may leave a strong enough positive impression that you will be sought out for future opportunities and positions.

Decision interviews

These interviews are typically conducted by the hiring manager or a team of individuals who have been given this responsibility. In many cases, these people are not well-trained interviewers and may therefore be even more nervous than you are in this process. You can do both of you a favor by being at ease, answering all questions honestly and directly, and asking a few good questions of your own. If you help keep the interview going, you'll make a good impression.

The hiring manager has three main concerns:

Can you do the job? This concern focuses on the question of skills and abilities. Do you have the required experience, education, and training to step into the position?

Will you do the job? This concern focuses on the question of desire and motivation. Do you want to perform and will you do what is required?

Will you fit into the organization? This concern addresses the issue of organizational culture and the other people with whom you will work. This is the "chemistry test." The manager wants to know: Will you fit in with the *family*?

As you interview, keep these three questions in mind and try to let everything you say reflect positively on what you *can do, will do,* and *how you will fit in*.

Asking you to attend a second or even a third decision interview is not cause for concern. The subsequent interviews may be with the hiring manager's superiors, other department managers, or other key people within the organization. Depending on the level of the position, the presidents of some companies like to *see* the finalist candidate. In many cases it is nothing more than a courtesy because the decision to hire you has already been made (although it should not be treated lightly or as if it has no significance). These interviews often last for only ten or fifteen minutes and may include no discussion about your qualifications. Answer any questions professionally and briefly, and thank the person for his or her time.

SEARCH TIP

Throughout your job search keep your focus on identifying your unique strengths as they relate to the needs of your potential employers.

Good Research Makes for Good Interviews

Before going to an interview, do enough research on the company—and, if you can, the position and the interviewer—to make yourself comfortable and knowledgeable. A company is much more than facts, history, products, and a balance sheet. You need to know what it's really like to work there. Is it formal or informal? Relaxed or pressurized? Do people actually talk to each other, or is everything communicated by memo and voice mail?

Before you interview, try to determine:

As much as you can about the company—its history, size, reputation in the industry, major product or service lines, and any major issues facing it today.

Who will be conducting the interview? Is it a screening or decision interview? What is the interviewer's position? Can he or she actually hire you?

Why is this job open? Did the last person to hold it quit after a few months? Or was he or she promoted?

How long has the position been open? Is it hard to fill? Or has the company only recently started looking?

Use your network to research the company and the interviewer. You can also obtain key information from your employment agency if you're using one. The company's own public relations and human resources departments can also provide important data and insights.

Arrive early. Ten minutes before the scheduled time is a good benchmark. Too early is almost as bad as too late. Use the ten minutes to use the restroom to straighten yourself out, use the facilities, and collect your composure. When you get to the interview, look around carefully. What do you see? Are people *chatting* in the halls? Are they smiling? Are they dressed informally? Or, is the atmosphere *strictly business*? Are people serious? How are people introduced—Bill and Mary, or Mr. Martin and Ms. Jacobs? These cues can tell you a lot about the organization.

Upon entering the interviewer's office, take a look around. A quick two- or three-second scan can give you some insights and knowledge about the interviewer. Are there pictures of family, pets, boats, or other things around? What types of books are on the shelves? Are there any knickknacks or other things on the desk or shelves? All of these things can be used as discussion starters and ice breakers. Most people don't jump right into the interview questions; there tends to be some small talk, and this can help build some rapport. How can you use this information to improve your interviewing activities?

Write out some thoughts:

_____

_____

_____

As you start the interview process, keep in mind the skills and other requirements for the job that you read in the advertisement or job description. You need to show your interviewer that your skills and traits are a good match for that position. You can do this by discussing your accomplishments in terms of the skills and traits that the company desires. Some examples:

THE COMPANY IS LOOKING FOR A CREATIVE PROBLEM SOLVER.

Weak Statement	Strong Accomplishment Statement
"I'm always looking for new ways to solve problems."	"Last summer I came up with a consolidated billing form that eliminated the need for several other forms."

THE COMPANY IS LOOKING FOR EXCELLENT COMMUNICATION SKILLS.

Weak Statement	Strong Accomplishment Statement
"I communicate well with people."	"In my volunteer position, I was able to attract four new patrons who contributed more than $20,000 to the museum."

It is a good idea to prepare more accomplishment statements than you actually have in your resume. This assures the interviewer that you have a wide range of desirable skills and traits.

Questions You Can Ask at On-site Interviews

Because interviewing is a two-way street, it is a good idea to prepare some of your own thoughtful questions that will communicate your interest and help you learn a lot more about the position and the company. Always put your questions in priority order, that is, in the order of most importance to you. The reason for putting them in order is because you may not be able to ask them all. Among the following group of questions, there are probably several you may want to ask at an appropriate time during your interview.

1. Why is this position open?

2. How large is the department, and to whom would I report?

3. Where did the last person in this job go? Why?

4. What are your immediate goals for the person who fills this opening?

5. What are your longer-term objectives for this position?

6. How long do people usually stay in this job?

7. How closely supervised would I be?

8. What equipment would I use? Would I be trained if it was unfamiliar?

9. What are the most difficult or frustrating parts of this position? How can those best be handled?

10. How are people promoted out of this job? Where do they typically go?

11. What changes do you foresee in the department and in the company?

12. Do you foresee any staff changes or downsizing in the near future?

13. What kind of person succeeds here?

14. What's the most important skill needed to do this job well?

15. What do you value most in an employee?

16. How do you handle employee problems?

17. How would you describe your management style?

18. How do you characterize the company's culture?

Are there any other questions that you can think of? List them in the space below.

_____

_____

_____

There are some subjects that should be avoided in the early stages of the interview process. These include vacation time, sick days, and coffee breaks. Mentioning them might make it seem that you are more interested in relaxation than in actually working. And above all, don't do what one candidate (who had recently been downsized) did in a screening interview. Within the first ten minutes of the interview, he asked, "Could you tell me about your severance package?" It may seem like common sense to avoid asking questions in these areas, but many candidates bring these things up and interview themselves out of a job. There is a time and a place to discuss these topics, but it comes later.

Sample Answers to Difficult Questions

You'll be more confident and relaxed in the interview if you practice good responses to difficult questions. If you're well prepared, you might even be disappointed if the interviewer doesn't ask you any "tough" questions. Following is a list of some of the most commonly asked questions—with suggested responses—to help prepare you for almost anything. (Note: Some questions may have more than one purpose.)

INTERVIEWER'S PURPOSE AND QUESTIONS

Purpose:	*Questions:*
Is this person prepared? Organized? Concise?	*1. Tell me about yourself.* Answer in about two minutes. Avoid minute details, don't ramble. Touch on these areas: education, types of jobs you've had, significant accomplishments, and current situation.
	2. Did you bring your resume?

INTERVIEWER'S PURPOSE AND QUESTIONS (*continued*)

Purpose:	*Questions:*

Yes. (Be prepared with two or three extra copies.)

3. What do you know about our organization?

Talk about the company's products, services, history, and people—especially friends and acquaintances who work there. You should also say, "But I would like to know more—particularly from your point of view. Do we have time to cover that now?"

4. According to your definition of success, how successful have you been so far?

Be prepared to define what you mean by success and then give some examples.

Is this person mature and self-aware?

5. What have been some of your most significant accomplishments?

Give one or two accomplishment statements. Don't take sole credit for team efforts but indicate that it was a team activity and explain your role.

6. Would you describe a few situations in which your work was criticized?

Purpose:	*Questions:*
	Give only one and tell how you have corrected (or plan to correct) the issue.

7. *What would the managers you've worked for say are your greatest strengths? Shortcomings or developmental areas?*

Be consistent with what you think these people would say. You never know whom the interviewer may know. Whenever possible, position the shortcoming in a positive way (refer to #10 below).

8. *How would you describe your personality?*

Keep your answers short and relevant to the position and the organization's culture. Don't give the interviewer superfluous information.

9. *What are your strong points?*

Present three and relate them to the organization and the position.

10. *What are your weak points?*

Don't say you have none. Think of areas that may be positives in disguise. For example: "I am sometimes impatient and do all the work myself when we are working

INTERVIEWER'S PURPOSE AND QUESTIONS *(continued)*

Purpose: *Questions:*

against tight deadlines," or "Sometimes I find myself helping others and extending my work day."

11. How did you do in school?

Emphasize your best and favorite courses or subject matter. If your grades were average, talk about your leadership activities or your team skills. You could also discuss how you worked to help finance your education.

Is this person motivated? What are his or her values, attitudes? Is there a fit?

12. What do you look for in a job?

Relate things you enjoy and find challenging in a work environment.

13. How long do you think it would take you to make a meaningful contribution to this organization?

Your response should indicate that the time frame will be relatively short but needs to be realistic. Your response may be something like, "Not long, I think, because of my experience, transferable skills, and ability to learn quickly."

14. How long would you stay with us?

A good response would include something like this: "As long as I

Purpose:	*Questions:*

feel I'm making a contribution and that my contribution is recognized."

15. If you have never supervised, how do you feel about assuming that responsibility?

Be honest in your response. If you don't want to supervise, emphasize that you can contribute more as an individual player. If you do want to supervise, say so and be enthusiastic.

16. Why do you want to become a supervisor?

Think about what is important to you. Your response might be something like: "To grow and develop professionally, to help others develop, to build a team, and to share what I have learned."

17. What do you see as the most difficult task in being a supervisor?

"Dealing with different personalities and getting things planned and done through others." If possible, show how you have done this in the past.

18. Describe your ideal working environment.

Refer to your ideal job profile. Relate it to this organization.

Purpose:	*Questions:*

19. Do you prefer working with figures or with words?

Be aware of what the job requires and position your answer (truthfully) in that context.

20. How would your co-workers/ fellow students/professors describe you?

Refer to your strengths and skills.

21. What do you think of your last boss?

If you liked him or her, say so and tell why. If you didn't, find something positive to say. Do not leave a negative impression.

22. Why do you want to work for a company this size? A company of this type?

Explain how this size and/or type of company works well for you—use examples from your past experiences if possible.

23. If you had your choice of jobs and companies, where would you go?

Acknowledge that no job is perfect. Give reasons why this job and this

Purpose:	*Questions:*

company are very close to what best suits you.

24. Why do you want to work for us?

Your response should focus on the fact that you would like to be part of a company project and to solve problems. You like what you've heard about this company, its policies, goals, and management: "I've researched the company and my friends tell me it's a very good place to work."

25. What was the last book you read? Movie you saw? Event you attended?

Think this one through. Your answer should be compatible with the company culture.

26. What kind of hours are you used to working?

Respond with "As many hours as it takes to get the job done." Then ask, "What is an average working day or week here?"

Does this person fit our job and criteria?

27. What would you do for us?

Relate past successes in problem solving that are similar to those of the prospective employer.

INTERVIEWER'S PURPOSE AND QUESTIONS (continued)

Purpose:	*Questions:*

28. What has your experience been in supervising people?

Give examples from your accomplishments.

29. How have you helped your previous employers?

Refer to your accomplishments.

30. What is the most money you have ever accounted for?

Refer to your accomplishments. If you haven't had budget responsibility, say so, but refer to an accomplishment that demonstrates the same skill and responsibility.

31. Describe some situations in which you have worked under pressure or had to meet deadlines.

Refer to accomplishments. Everyone who graduates from college is familiar with pressure and deadlines.

32. Give an example of your creativity.

Refer to your accomplishments.

33. Give examples of your leadership abilities.

Purpose:	*Questions:*

Draw examples from your accomplishments.

34. What are your career goals?

Talk first about succeeding in the job for which you are applying, then talk about longer-range plans.

35. What position do you expect to have in two years?

"A position similar to the one we are discussing, or the next step up." However, you don't want to come across as overly ambitious and unrealistic, nor do you want to be perceived as lacking ambition and complacent.

36. What are your objectives?

Refer to question #34 on goals. Keep long-range answers fairly general. Your responses should have a short-range, specific focus. Talk about particular skills you want to master, growth opportunities, maybe having more responsibilities, or moving into management.

How does this person handle stress? What is his or her confidence level?

37. Why should we hire you?

Relate a past experience in successful problem solving that may be similar to those of the prospective employer.

INTERVIEWER'S PURPOSE AND QUESTIONS (continued)

Purpose:	*Questions:*
	38. *Why haven't you found a position before now?*
	"Finding the right job takes time. I'm not looking for just *any* job. And I think you know what the job market for recent graduates is like today."
	39. *How much salary do you expect if we offer you this position?*
	Be very careful in responding to this question. If you don't know the market value of the position, return the question by saying that you would expect a fair salary based on the job's responsibilities, your experience, skills, and education. Ask what salary range has been set for the position. If you know the market value of the job, that may be the key answer, "My understanding is that a job like this one may be in the range of $ _____. Is that in your ball park?" Whenever possible, get the interviewer to put a salary figure on the table first. You should have a target range in mind so that you can respond to the suggested amount.
What is this person's market value?	40. *What kind of salary are you worth?*

Purpose:	*Questions:*

Again, whenever possible, get the interviewer to put a salary figure on the table first, but have a target range in mind.

Ask more about specific responsibilities of the job. This will tell you how important the job is to the company. When the interviewer opens the *real* discussion of salary, you will be in a much better position to determine what the job is worth to both the employer and to you. Delay all mention of money until the end of the interview. If the interviewer insists on a number, quote a range. But be careful not to make the range too narrow or too broad. A $3,000 to $5,000 difference between the high and low is usually appropriate.

41. What other types of jobs or companies are you considering?

"I'm looking at similar positions in several companies." You don't have to be specific in terms of position titles or names of companies. It may seem awkward at first, but practicing aloud is the best way to rehearse your answers. It's one thing to *think* about what you'll say to a given question, it's quite another to actually *say* it while observing yourself being observed

INTERVIEWER'S PURPOSE AND QUESTIONS (*continued*)

Purpose:	*Questions:*
	for feedback. You can practice with someone else, by yourself in front of a mirror, or with an audio tape recorder or video camera. If the latter two are available, use them. The practice will pay off.

While reviewing your practice interview, pay attention to:

What you say— the actual meaning you convey.

How you say it— your choice of words, words you omit, and how you build your case. For instance, "I do best in a flexible environment" is preferable to "I hated the petty rules and regulations at my last job."

Body language and tone of voice (your nonverbal communication actions)—do they support what you are saying or do they contradict your words? Keep in mind that when the nonverbal communication conflicts with the verbal (the words you speak) communication, the nonverbal will win out most of the time. If you claim to be energetic and motivated, speak with conviction and sit forward on your chair. It would be hard for an interviewer to believe you if you rarely talked above a whisper and leaned back in your chair during the interview.

What to bring to the interview

- **Briefcase or folder** to hold and protect your papers.

- **Your resume**—actually bring several extra copies in case the interviewer can't find his or her copy. You'll also want to have one to refer to yourself. Your own data sheet to help you complete the employment application quickly.

- **A notebook, appointment calendar, and a pen** to jot down important information or to schedule your next interview with the company. (Don't take extensive notes during the interview, however. This precludes good eye contact and will distract your attention from what is being said.)

- **Weather-related accessories.** If you forget your umbrella and are caught in a downpour, you won't look very professional.

Be Early

The only way to make sure you'll be on time is to allow plenty of extra time for the unexpected. Remember Murphy's Law: "Whatever can go wrong will go wrong." If nothing does, you'll be early—allowing you time to catch your breath, read over your resume at a relaxed pace, and to introduce yourself to the secretary or receptionist. Being early also gives you a moment to check your appearance in a mirror and tend to any grooming needs that will make you feel more self-confident. It is always a good idea to use the restroom prior to meeting the interviewer.

Take time to be friendly. Get the receptionist's or secretary's name and make some light conversation. Practice projecting confidence when you speak. Even though this person may not have a lot of influence with the boss (though you shouldn't assume this), you'll be able to hear your own voice. This can help relax you. And it may help you to get through to the hiring manager with follow-up phone calls.

If you have a coat, umbrella, or other bulky items, ask if you can leave them out front with the receptionist so you won't be burdened when you meet the interviewer. Pay attention to your breathing during the time you're waiting. Deep breaths will make you feel more relaxed. Waiting also gives you the opportunity to survey the office environment. Get a feeling of what kind of place it is. You may be able to overhear office conversations (but don't appear to be actively listening). All these cues and clues can help you assess the office atmosphere.

Make a Good First Impression

During the first few seconds of an interview, while you are still meeting the interviewer and getting seated and ready to go, you'll be conveying some impressions that often lead the interviewer to reach a conclusion about you. It's far easier to build on this first impression than to turn it around. That's why a good, positive first impression is so important. And remember the importance of a firm handshake.

Dress to your advantage in a style that's consistent with the type of position for which you are applying. Conservative dress is always appropriate. Of course, there could be jobs for which a more flamboyant style would fit perfectly. In northern and metropolitan areas, dark, conservative attire is usually safest. In more rural areas, less formal—even sporty—clothing may be appropriate. Check into the style of dress in this new work community, particularly in the organization where you're interviewing.

The objective is to fit the environment where you'd like to work. Naturally, you'll want to be sure your shoes are polished and your hair and nails are well groomed. Jewelry should be sparse. Women's makeup should be appropriate for business.

Interview rooms tend to be small, so go easy on the perfume or after-shave. A deodorant or antiperspirant is a wise bet for this nervous occasion. And if you're having a meal before the interview, skip the garlic, spicy foods, and alcohol.

If you're a smoker, forget it. Smoking today is *verboten* in most office environments. And gum-chewing just isn't appropriate to the situation. If you must, smoke or chew outside the building—before you introduce yourself to the receptionist.

As you have read, there are many things that need to be considered in the interview process. Some are readily apparent, but many are too subtle to recognize. Consider the following situations:

When you arrive for your interview you are greeted by a receptionist. How do you behave toward her or him? Are you just as friendly as you plan to be with the hiring manager? Is it possible that the hiring manager will ask for some feedback from the receptionist regarding how you reacted? You'd better believe it!

You arrive about ten minutes early for your interview. A receptionist greets you in a friendly, courteous manner and walks you down the hall to the hiring manager's office. The two of you engage in "friendly conversation" for about twenty minutes. What has taken place? Would you believe that it was planned, and that you were being interviewed? Well, it was and you were.

You have your first interview of the day with the human resources professional or the hiring manager. Before leaving this person's office, you are given a coffee mug with the corporate logo to take with you. What is your sense of this? One company gave all the *rejects* coffee mugs to let the other interviewers know that they should not spend too much time with these candidates. Unfortunately, the candidates had no idea what the mug symbolized. Don't think that if you are given a coffee mug that it *always* means that you are no longer a viable candidate, but it is a possibility.

You leave the hiring manager's office. Is the interview over? No way. You will be judged and evaluated until you are out of sight—by the way you talk, the way you act, and how you carry yourself.

As a friendly gesture, the hiring manager, or perhaps an administrative assistant, walks you out to your car in the parking lot. What is your reaction? This is a very friendly place. In some instances they are looking at how you take care of your car—is it clean, is it neat inside? What can be inferred by looking at how you take care of your car?

THE DINING INTERVIEW

Some hiring managers like to interview over meals—breakfast, lunch, or dinner. In many cases a mealtime interview cannot be avoided because it happens right in the middle of the interview schedule. It is not a horrendous fate, but it certainly needs to be handled with care.

Meals present other obstacles in the interview process. There are some things to think about when it comes to dining and interviewing. How are your table manners and etiquette? What do you order? Should you have an alcoholic beverage? The list can go on and on.

A few true examples to demonstrate. An individual was being interviewed for a senior position in a high-tech firm. The position would require the candidate to meet with customers and clients at social gatherings and over dinner at least once or twice a month. The appropriate candidate needed to have excellent technical skills in a specific area. This meant that there were not a lot of people who were available with the appropriate qualifications. Over dinner, this highly competent (from a technical perspective) individual spoke with his mouth full, to the point where small bits of food were projected onto the table near the hiring manager. There was no doubt in the mind of the manager that this person was probably one of the two or three most qualified people for the job, but there was also no doubt that he would not be hired. Poor etiquette and table manners were the downfall of this candidate.

A candidate was being interviewed over lunch in an Italian restaurant. It was summer and she was wearing a beige business suit. She ordered spaghetti and meatballs for lunch. While she was attempting to cut the meatball, it somehow jumped into the air and landed on her lapel, rolled down the front of her jacket (leaving a red racing stripe), and onto the floor, where it was promptly squished by a passing waiter. She was so unnerved by the incident that she was unable to continue the interview.

One company always takes its candidates for sales positions to a steakhouse. The company has an agreement with the manager of the restaurant to cook the candidate's steak just the opposite of what is ordered. The purpose is to see what the candidate will do—to check his or her assertiveness.

In the *Wall Street Journal*, Monday, February 27, 1995, in an article entitled "Doomed Days" (p. R4), an executive recruiter, Richard Slayton of Slayton International, Inc. Chicago, relates the following: "Over dinner with the president of my client company, a senior executive at a major office-communications company was interviewing for a top post. When the dinner was over, the candidate made a big mistake by asking for a doggie bag."

Good Rules for Mealtime Interviews:

- Try to avoid a mealtime interview whenever possible.

- Always order light, even if you are very hungry.

- Never order anything that could splash—for example, spaghetti sauce.

- Never order alcohol, even if your host is ordering a drink. It could diminish your capacity to answer the interview questions as well as you would like.

- Don't order the most expensive or the least expensive item on the menu.

Being well prepared for your interview lets you focus your attention on the interview and the interviewer. If you aren't distracted and if you haven't forgotten something, you'll be far better able to concentrate on the matter at hand. Pleasing the customer is the goal of all marketing efforts. This is your marketing effort for *you*. And you'll need to pay full attention to your customer, the interviewer. Getting off to a good start is essential. And you have only this one chance to do it right.

A firm handshake, a genuine smile, and good eye contact go a long way toward creating a positive first impression. Wait for the interviewer to sit down or offer you a chair before taking a seat yourself. If you're not sure where to sit, ask.

The Dialogue

There's no need to blurt out your best and most significant attributes the minute you sit down. Let the conversation develop naturally. It will likely take you and the interviewer a few minutes to become comfortable with each other, to establish some rapport, and to bring your concentration to the matter at hand. A little small talk is appropriate—the weather, last night's sports score. Remember what we said earlier about scanning the office. You need to be observant. But it's best to let the interviewer initiate the small talk. Try to get the interviewer to talk about himself or herself early. This will give you a better idea of his or her interests and style of communicating. But don't be pushy. Let the interviewer control the conversation. And *never* interrupt in your eagerness to get a point across.

If you need some help with identifying the speaking and, perhaps, the thinking styles of other people and ways to interact appropriately with each style, Drake Beam Morin, Inc. (DBM) has a proprietary program entitled *I-Speak Your Language©*. This program is based on the research of Dr. Carl Jung, the noted Swiss psychologist. Jung's studies reveal that everyone has four styles of communication available, but one style tends to dominate. Familiarity with the four styles allows you to recognize your own and other people's styles. And this familiarity will give you a quick sense of how to communicate with others most effectively. Jung's work is also the basis for the Myers-Briggs Type Indicator, referred to earlier.

For more information on I-Speak Your Language©, contact DBM toll-free at 800-345-JOBS.

The Heart of the Interview

You have a limited amount of time to "make the sale" in an interview. Remember your objective: convince the customer—through an honest and positive presentation and by establishing good rapport—that you are the best candidate for the job. And use your time wisely.

You will come across as a strong candidate if you answer questions positively and succinctly, relating your skills and experience to job requirements. Get as much information about the position as you can early in the interview. Using this information, you can highlight your related experiences and avoid volunteering information that is not relevant. By providing brief and informative answers, you allow the interviewer to steer the discussion, asking about the things that most interest him or her.

Be sure you understand a question before attempting to answer it. You want to address the interviewer's particular concerns. If the question is not clear, ask for clarification rather than guessing what is meant. This simple approach can prevent you from getting off on the wrong track. Also, in answering briefly, it's fine to ask if you have answered the question sufficiently or whether the interviewer would like more detail. This question allows you to use your time wisely and to address only those issues of importance to the interviewer. As with all interview techniques, don't overuse either of these approaches. Use your own good judgment in both presenting information and requesting or offering clarification.

Relating your ability and experience to the job in question is the strongest sales argument there is. Relate your actual accomplishments proudly, and you will be less likely to find yourself bragging or claiming you can do anything. Sticking to the relevant facts will make both you and the interviewer more comfortable.

You'll also come across well by presenting information in a positive light and avoiding negatives. It's especially important to be positive—as well as brief—in discussing your reasons for seeking work in a particular geographic area and your past work experiences including part-time and summer jobs while in school. Talk in terms of challenges rather than problems. Briefly describe what job-related opportunities the job offers you. And avoid, at all costs, any long story portraying the horrors of past employers or positions. Religion and politics are two more inappropriate and dangerous topics. Name-dropping is considered politics. Unless you met the interviewer through a mutual acquaintance within the company, it's best not to mention the other person's name. It could work against you as easily as in your favor.

As we said earlier, salary can be controversial. If you can delay a discussion of money until the end of the interview, do so. If you're asked early on about your minimum requirement, try to counter with your need to learn more about the scope of the job. Your negotiating position will be stronger after you've sold the interviewer that you're the person the company needs. However, don't let the issue of whether to discuss salary become a point of controversy. Be prepared to state the range of your salary expectations at any point in the interview. This range should be based on comparative data for this type of position, at your level of experience, within this industry.

Interviews can be more enjoyable and productive for both you and the person across the desk if you can sustain a meaningful dialogue. Continue to ask appropriate questions during the heart of the interview. Learn about the interviewer's views. And watch for opportunities to ask questions that demonstrate that you've done some research on the company.

Monitor the tone of the discussion. If it should become negative, try to change it. Ask a tactful question or try to introduce another relevant topic. This is not the time for being either critical or argumentative. The interviewer, remember, is your customer. And you know what they say about customers!

Ending the Interview

Try to end the interview on a positive note. If the dialogue has been enjoyable, say so. If your discussion has made you enthusiastic about the position, let the interviewer know. Genuine enthusiasm may help you win the interview . . . and the job. Everyone wants to work with people who are both qualified and positive.

At the end of most interviews, many interviewers will ask if you have any further questions. If you do, ask them. If you don't, express your appreciation for the interviewer's time, and express your genuine interest in the position you've been discussing. Then, you might add something like, "I'm very interested in this position. Could you give me a general idea of how my qualifications and background fit with your concept of the 'ideal candidate'?" A question like this is far better than, "Well, what do you think? How did I do?"

Before you leave, make sure you understand the next steps. If no specific arrangement has been established to contact you, ask when the organization expects to make some preliminary evaluation. Then propose a date for contacting the interviewer. There is no need to be defensive about this. Interviewers sometimes simply forget to tie up the loose ends. And, you're demonstrating follow-through, which is a good business practice. Always ask everyone you interview with for a business card, unless one has already been received. This way you'll be absolutely certain of the spelling of the interviewer's name and organizational title. You'll need this information for your thank-you note.

Interviewing Do's and Don'ts

Don't ramble; be succinct.

Stop talking when you have answered the question. Too many candidates talk themselves out of a job.

After you're asked a question, take a moment before you answer.

Be sure you hear the question, then respond to it directly.

Use positive terms when responding to all questions.

Maintain good eye contact (not staring) with your interviewer, and smile appropriately.

Seize opportunities to point out how you could help your new employer.

Avoid sounding mechanical in your answers; sound thoughtful.

Don't "overanswer"—giving too much information can be worse than giving too little.

The corollary to this is simple: Be brief.

Don't promise too much.

Don't argue with the interviewer.

Don't let the interviewer ask all the questions; take part in a dialogue.

Don't let a few moments of silence make you say the wrong thing.

Be honest in your answers.

Try to relax.

Ed Ryan, president of Marketing Personnel Research, Inc., a Chicago-based worldwide consulting firm specializing in productivity improvement by selection and management of talented people for all positions within an organization, indicates, "Many companies still look at experience as the key factor in making hiring decisions, and the problems facing a lot of students is that they don't have the experience employers desire." In order to assess some of this experience, according to Mr. Ryan, "more and more companies are moving toward a behavioral assessment of candidates."

Learning how to have a successful interview is only part of the equation. You need to have the skills and abilities to do the job. Mr. Ryan goes on to say, "A concern that I have is that some people are teaching students how to *beat* an interview. We may put them in a position where they could fail. I wouldn't want to see that; we have enough failure experiences in life as it is."

CHAPTER 9

Negotiating the Job Offer

WHAT IS NEGOTIABLE?

Many recent graduates seeking their first career position don't believe they're in a position to negotiate anything. A common attitude seems to be, "Negotiating is only for top people, especially in a tight job market; people at our level take what's offered." However, that just isn't the case—even today. Though the salary may be a given (and many times, it isn't), there are other aspects of a job that can be negotiated. So most things can be negotiated.

Negotiation is not simply bargaining about salary; it is the process through which you and the employer agree on the terms of your employment. These terms can be broken down into four parts:

The job— its title or level, responsibilities, location, any duties for supervising others or managing projects, reporting relationships, and opportunities for advancement.

Conditions of employment— your start date, work schedule, travel requirements, and opportunities for flex time.

Benefits— such as vacation time, sick pay, health and life insurance, corporate-paid child care, tuition reimbursement, and much more.

Salary— including your starting salary, the frequency of salary reviews, and any bonuses.

Here's a list of things that can often be negotiated:

Compensation:

Base salary

Overtime

Sales commissions

Bonuses

Money in place of benefits

Benefits:

"Cafeteria" benefit plan

Personal days off

Perquisites:

Flexible schedule ("flex time")

Expense account

Carfare reimbursement

Liberal gas allowance

Free lunches

Company-paid (or sponsored) child care

Severance provisions:

Outplacement services

Severance settlement

Insurance programs:

Medical

Dental

Life

Long-term disability

Financial programs:

Stock options

Company-paid pension/annuity

Corporate performance

Participation plan

Matching investment/profit sharing programs

401K plan

Thrift plan

Employee services:

Annual physical exam

Legal, tax, financial assistance

Loans and mortgages at reduced rates

Discounts on purchases:

Computer equipment

Word processing

Free company services (free checking from a bank, etc.)

On-premises health club

Educational programs:

Tuition reimbursement

Education/training expenses

Professional association memberships

Because you are negotiating for a "mix" of these items, you should know what is most important to you. Do not assume just because you are an entry-level employee that a seemingly "executive" benefit is not available to you. Explore all options—tactfully, of course.

You might want to go over this list of negotiable items and mark each one with an **A, B,** or **C**. Those you mark **A** are essential (**A**bsolutely necessary)—you truly believe you must have these. **B** items (**B**eneficial) are important but not essential. And **C** items (**C**onvenient) are less important and can be traded for other items that are more important. However, keep your **A** list short if you haven't had much full-time work experience. Don't end up sounding presumptuous or foolish by coming in with a laundry list of demands. Determine items that are likely negotiable by asking the advice of a company "insider" or a career counselor.

What must you have? You may require a minimum salary level or carfare allowance. If these requirements are not part of the offer, you should be prepared to turn the position down or go back to the drawing board and review what you truly must have. (In addition to your minimum acceptable salary, you should also have a desired salary in mind.)

What is important? Health or some other type of insurance? These items are desirable but not essential. You may be prepared to be flexible on one of these items to get one of your "must have" items.

"Opportunities are disguised as hard work, so most people don't recognize them."
—Ann Landers

What is less important? A longer vacation? A higher sales commission? You can easily be flexible on—or even give up—one of these items in exchange for a higher priority item.

Know What the Employer Is Willing to Offer

Use your networking contacts to get a good idea of the salary range for entry-level positions such as the one you're seeking—within your industry and, if possible, within the company you're interviewing. Does the company have a "job grade system?" What job grades apply to this job, and what are the high and low salaries for each grade? How flexible is the company (and the boss) on other important items such as flex time, commuting allowances, personal leave, and overtime?

If you can't learn this information through networking, you can ask these questions at some point during a subsequent interview. Negotiations begin only after a firm job offer is made by the employer. Don't try to start negotiating before you have the offer. In fact, before the offer, it's usually a good idea not to mention salary at all. Instead, as we stated earlier, wait for the interviewer to bring it up.

Some Guidelines for Negotiating

Decision interviews

Informal negotiations usually begin here as the employer sizes up what you can contribute to the organization and you estimate your worth to this employer. It is still too early to begin formal negotiations because the employer is not sure that he or she wants to extend an offer, and the job may not yet have been fully defined. You can't arrive at a compensation level when you don't know the exact job responsibilities or the company's established performance standards.

If you have had a comparable full-time position recently and the interviewer asks what you were making—or if you're asked what your expected salary is at this early stage—you might say, "Could we get back to that after I learn more about the responsibilities of the position?" If the interviewer persists, you can respond with, "I know the salary range at some other companies, but I don't know yours. What is the range for this position?" Another approach is to say to the interviewer, "Based upon the requirements of the position and my background and skills, what would be an appropriate compensation level?" Whatever you do at this stage, avoid quoting an actual figure. If the number is too high, you may price yourself out of the market. If the figure is too low, the employer will know he or she doesn't have to offer you a nickel more. Some interviewers, hearing a low-ball figure, may think you are underqualified for the position. So ask for a range. And if you're pressed, respond with a range yourself. The figure you're trying to get to should be somewhere in the middle of the range. For example, if you're looking for $25,000, you might say you're looking at positions in the $22,000–to–$27,500 range. The range for positions under $40,000 should be $3,000 to 5,000 and $7,000 to 10,000 for positions targeted at over $40,000.

"Only one person in the whole world can defeat you. That is yourself."
—ANONYMOUS

Try to get the interviewer to show his or her cards first. Negotiating is a lot like playing poker: the player who shows his or her cards first is at a disadvantage. That's why you ask the interviewer for a range before giving one yourself. During the decision interview stage, you can strengthen your negotiating position by concentrating on building value and looking for signals of an offer.

Building value

When you enter an interview room, your value to the potential employer hasn't yet been established. Throughout the interview, you can build that value by discussing your accomplishments—particularly those that apply to your potential employer's situation. Later, when it's time to make an offer, the employer will be more likely to be flexible on compensation or terms of employment in order to hire a valuable addition to the staff. If you've never had a full-time job, choose accomplishments from academic life or part-time jobs that indicate you have skills valuable to the employer. These might include organizational skills and demonstrated leadership ability.

Reading the signals of an offer

There are definite signals that indicate you have established your value to the company, and that the firm is now seriously considering making you an offer. Some of these include:

The interview runs longer than planned.

You are asked back for a second or third interview.

The interviewer tries to "sell" you on the company.

The interviewer is very specific about salary, benefits, and/or a start date.

The interviewer says he or she will call your references soon.

The interviewer wants you to meet his or her boss or someone else of higher authority.

Negotiating the Job Offer

The secret to negotiating any job offer is to negotiate more than one dimension—salary, benefits, bonuses, vacation, etc. When you receive an offer, don't respond immediately. The position won't evaporate if you ask for a day or two to think the offer over. Employers know that some new grads may have several offers, and most will give you some decision time. Thank the interviewer or whomever makes you the offer, then ask for a meeting to discuss it further. As you go over each part of the package you've been offered, use your list of **A, B,** and **C** items to determine how you really feel about it and how it fits with your true needs. Most employers will give you a job offer in writing. If not, ask for one in writing. This is especially important if you are going to leave one job for another.

If a job offer meets your expectations, your decision should be fairly easy. However, if the offer is borderline, you may need to ask yourself some questions:

- Are my original guidelines realistic or should I modify them?

- Have I really used up all my good leads . . . and is this the best offer I'm likely to get?

- How long would it take to find new job leads? Good ones?

- How are my money and my patience holding out? Should I take this job and start looking for a better one when I've gained some experience and am financially more stable?

Remember that negotiating is not arguing! Ask to review and discuss all parts of the offer with the person who made it—with the intent of arriving at an agreement that is satisfactory to you both. You may wind up working for this person, and if you negotiate too aggressively, it may affect that working relationship. Always remain calm, friendly, and flexible. If an employer says an item is not negotiable, go on to another one.

Accepting or Rejecting an Offer

When you receive a verbal offer you want to accept, it's a good idea to find out if there are other conditions to meet before you are employed—such as a medical exam, drug test, or further reference checks. In addition, you should discuss your understanding of the employment agreement with the hiring manager to make sure major points are mutually understood. Ask for a written offer that contains the major points you have agreed on. If this is not the company's policy, write your own letter to the company (addressed to the hiring manager) outlining the agreement and your acceptance of the job. Keep a copy of this letter in case there are any misunderstandings later on.

"If you think you can, or if you think you can't, you're right."

—Anonymous

If you decide to reject an offer, don't burn your bridges. This is especially true if you've spent a lot of time negotiating with the company. Phone the person who extended the offer, explain why you are declining, and follow up with a brief note of appreciation. (It is well to remember that you may wind up working for this company later in your career.) You also never know whom this person may know. If you are rejecting an offer because the salary is too low, there's a chance the company may get back to you with a better figure or package. Keep your options open, though, and continue your job search until you actually begin your new job.

Cost of Living Comparisons

In starting their careers, many recent graduates move to a new city—either by choice or because the job happens to be there. But it's important to remember that the buying power of a given income depends to a large degree on where you live. This makes it prudent to consider a city's cost of living in order to determine whether a given salary will actually meet your needs.

The American Chamber of Commerce Researchers Association publishes the *Inter-City Cost of Living Index* on a quarterly basis. Some examples of their findings measure relative price levels for consumer goods and services, which can be found on the following pages. To compare two cities, use the index percentage number for each city and plug them into this equation:

$$\frac{(City\ \#1)}{(City\ \#2)} \quad \frac{Index\ \#\ \times\ salary}{Index\ \#} \quad = \quad \$$$

How much does a person in Atlanta need to earn annually to have the buying power of someone making $25,000 a year in San Diego?

$$\frac{Atlanta}{San\ Diego} \quad \frac{97.2\ \times\ \$25,000}{122.3} \quad = \quad \$19,869$$

How much does a person in San Diego need to earn annually to have the buying power of someone making $25,000 a year in Atlanta?

$$\frac{\text{San Diego}}{\text{Atlanta}} \quad \frac{122.3 \times \$25,000}{97.2} = \$31,456$$

COST OF LIVING INDEX BY STATE AND MAJOR CITY

ALABAMA

Birmingham	99.1
Huntsville	95.1

ALASKA

Anchorage	126.5

ARIZONA

Phoenix	101.2
Tucson	99.7

ARKANSAS

Fort Smith	89.1
Little Rock	87.2

CALIFORNIA

Bakersfield	107.6
Los Angeles	123.9
Palm Springs	116.0
San Diego	122.3

COLORADO

Boulder	111.8
Colorado Springs	96.8
Denver	104.5

CONNECTICUT

Hartford	123.7

DELAWARE

Wilmington	110.3

DISTRICT OF COLUMBIA

Washington, DC	132.4

FLORIDA

Jacksonville	94.9
Miami	107.8
Orlando	98.5
Tampa	94.9
West Palm Beach	110.3

GEORGIA

Atlanta	97.2

IDAHO

Boise	101.4

ILLINOIS

Bloomington	102.8
Champaign	102.3
Peoria	97.0

COST OF LIVING INDEX BY STATE AND MAJOR CITY (continued)

INDIANA

Indianapolis	97.4
South Bend	91.5

IOWA

Cedar Rapids	100.8
Des Moines	96.9

KANSAS

Lawrence	93.8
Wichita	94.8

KENTUCKY

Lexington	99.2
Louisville	91.5

LOUISIANA

Baton Rouge	100.2
New Orleans	95.8

MARYLAND

Baltimore	103.1
Hagerstown	97.8

MASSACHUSETTS

Boston	137.7

MICHIGAN

Grand Rapids	102.1
Lansing	104.2

MINNESOTA

    Minneapolis–St. Paul   101.5

MISSISSIPPI

    Jackson   95.2

MISSOURI

    Kansas City   95.0
    St. Louis   97.8

MONTANA

    Billings   103.4

NEBRASKA

    Lincoln   90.5
    Omaha   92.1

NEVADA

    Las Vegas   109.0
    Reno/Sparks   111.9

NEW HAMPSHIRE

    Manchester   111.6

NEW MEXICO

    Albuquerque   103.4
    Santa Fe   121.7

NEW YORK

    Albany   107.1
    Binghamton   97.1

COST OF LIVING INDEX BY STATE AND MAJOR CITY (*continued*)

New York City	128.3
Syracuse	104.6
NORTH CAROLINA	
Charlotte	98.7
Raleigh/Durham	98.0
Winston–Salem	97.5
NORTH DAKOTA	
Bismarck	102.1
OHIO	
Cincinnati	101.0
Cleveland	104.3
Columbus	104.3
OKLAHOMA	
Oklahoma City	92.9
Tulsa	91.0
OREGON	
Eugene	111.8
Portland	109.7
Salem	103.2
PENNSYLVANIA	
Allentown	104.6
Harrisburg	104.9
Lancaster	104.3
Philadelphia	127.8

SOUTH CAROLINA

Charleston	98.1

SOUTH DAKOTA

Rapid City	97.4
Sioux Falls	96.6

TENNESSEE

Memphis	96.1
Nashville	94.6

TEXAS

Amarillo	91.1
Dallas	101.9
El Paso	94.2
Fort Worth	93.7
Houston	97.0
Lubbock	92.3
San Antonio	94.9

UTAH

Provo/Orem	96.8
Salt Lake City	108.0

VERMONT

Burlington	113.2
Montpelier	108.1

VIRGINIA

Richmond	100.9
Roanoke	91.3

COST OF LIVING INDEX BY STATE AND MAJOR CITY (continued)

WASHINGTON

Bellingham	104.2
Seattle	108.1
Tacoma	104.0

WEST VIRGINIA

Charleston	98.0
Martinsburg	91.8

WISCONSIN

Eau Claire	103.4
Green Bay	96.9
Milwaukee	103.4

WYOMING

Casper	104.0
Cheyenne	96.6

SOURCE: American Chamber of Commerce Researchers Association, *Inter-City Cost of Living Index*, Fourth Quarter 1994.

NOTE: This index, produced by the American Chamber of Commerce Researchers Association, is updated quarterly and reflects the cost of housing, transportation, health care, and various consumer items, but it excludes taxes. Cities listed here are those with chambers of commerce that volunteered to participate in the survey.

CHAPTER 10

After You're Hired:

Survival Strategies for Your New Job

Congratulations! You've worked hard and you've won your first real (or next) career position—the job of your choice. Now you will want to take a few minutes to think about succeeding in that job and preparing . . . yes, beginning even now . . . for your next position. Because what you do in and with this job, beginning your first day, will determine—to an unexpected degree—what and *where* that next job will be.

FIRST, THE BASICS

At the close of your final meeting prior to actually starting your new job, make sure you get the following information:

The job's location, work hours, and the name of your immediate supervisor.

What employment papers you need to complete—

sometimes these can be filled out before you actually report for work.

Whether the company typically announces new employees' names, positions, and backgrounds— perhaps in a newsletter or press release. If so, ask if your employment can be so announced.

If the company or organization has an employee handbook, try to obtain a copy so that you can read it over before actually starting to work.

Be sure you are at least on time—early is better—the first day on the job. Ask your boss or a co-worker what the customs and practices are concerning any break times, lunch time, and when the day ends for your group or department. And dress the part of a professional person reporting for a new position. The dress code in some organizations today can be pretty relaxed. Find out what is appropriate. If it seems your wardrobe isn't quite up to the culture of your new company, it might be wise to invest in some new clothes. And, by the way, that is what you'll be doing—investing in yourself and in your future. The whole idea is to look, act, and conduct yourself as the person you seek to become. Do that consistently and you will *become* that person.

"Do not let what you cannot do interfere with what you can do."

—ANONYMOUS

Try to learn what became of the person who held your position before you were hired. Was he or she promoted?

Terminated? Did the person quit? The fate of your predecessor isn't necessarily tied to your own in any way.

"Never, never, never quit."
—WINSTON CHURCHILL

Getting Off to the Right Start with Your Boss

Your relationship with your immediate supervisor is the most important relationship you're going to encounter. What is your boss's communication style? How does he or she think and consistently express himself or herself? Identifying the communication style can go a long way to helping you communicate more clearly, precisely, and convincingly with your supervisor. Another thing: some people prefer to have things in writing; others prefer to hear the same types of things orally. Try to determine your manager's type. This will give you important insight into how you should present ideas, issues, questions, and problems more effectively to this person. It is an excellent idea to ask for a brief meeting with your immediate supervisor early on to make certain you are in alignment on your job responsibilities, duties, and priorities. You should have a reasonably good idea of these based on your interviews. Sometimes it makes sense for you and your boss both to fill out a list of the five most important things for you to concentrate on doing. When you compare your lists, at least three of the items should be the same. If they aren't, ask for guidance and direction.

Ascertain what your group's practice is concerning performance reviews. These regular sessions with your boss help you understand how your activities and results compare with his or her expectations. In many companies, performance reviews are held annually, and in some they are conducted semiannually. During your first six months or so, you might suggest an informal meeting every two or three months until you have begun to settle in to the new job. And you might mark your calendar so that you can remind your boss—in writing—a day or two before the appointed date. During the performance review, you will want to discuss what has gone well, any problems you've encountered, and how you've resolved them. You should expect the supervisor's honest appraisal of your work and recommendations for improvement. If you don't get these, ask tactfully for them.

"Well done is better than well said."
—BEN FRANKLIN

Relationships

Getting along with co-workers—at all levels—is essential. Not only is it essential to success in your position and in your career, but you'll find good working relationships increasingly important to your happiness on the job and your satisfaction as an employee. Being friendly, helpful, cooperative, and willing to "dig in" and do your share are all traits that will win high marks among those with whom you'll be working.

Be careful about office politics; they can be deadly. Until you truly know the territory, it's best to avoid joining any cliques. You might also be justifiably wary of any one person who seems to seek you out with great vigor. There may be some ulterior motive at work there. You can hardly go wrong if you're cordial and friendly with everyone.

"Success is a journey, not a destination."
—BEN SWEETLAND

It's fine to be sociable, too. Lunch dates with colleagues, dinner parties at someone's home, working together on charitable or professional projects are all excellent means for getting to know your associates and your organization better. And while norms of "togetherness" in companies do vary, social occasions provide the opportunity to gain a lot of useful information and to get the kind of exposure that can move your career forward.

Avoid overtly competitive behaviors toward other people. In college, you were on your own most of the time. In this environment, people get work done by working together—in concert if not actually in tandem. The "team player" may be a cliché, but such a person is still highly valued. You will further your own career if you can become a good one. In fact, more and more organizations are becoming team-oriented, not only in the way that work gets done but also in terms of how employees are compensated. Your future compensation may be determined by how well your team succeeds in achieving its goals.

Learn who has the power. Sometimes it's not where an outsider would think it is. The administrative assistant who is the real power behind the boss is more typical than you might believe. Before you *know* who has the power, be wary of crossing anyone. *After* you know, it's still best not to cross anyone. A good lesson to learn is to become friendly with two groups of people who can make or break your future success. The two groups are clerical/administrative and maintenance. If you don't, the report that urgently needs to be word-processed ends up on the bottom of the pile, not the top, and the conference room that needs to be cleaned is not prepared for that meeting with an important client. And there will always be a legitimate reason why it was not done.

Two final words

Have fun! You've come a long way since graduation. You've put a lot of time and effort into securing the position that will launch your career. There's a lot riding on this job. So put everything you've got into doing it to the very best of your ability; no one can ask for more. And remember, too—there's a great ride ahead.

There's just no telling where or how high you can go in your career. The sky is truly the limit for enthusiastic, well-educated, highly motivated and skilled people in the workplace of the '90s and beyond.

You've got a great life ahead. Enjoy it!

Bibliography

This is not a comprehensive list of available publications, but it will give you a place to start and supplement this publication.

Adams, Bob. *The Complete Resume & Job Search Book for College Students*. Holbrook, MA: Adams Publishing, 1992.

Boldt, Laurence G. *Zen and the Art of Making a Living*. New York: The Penguin Group, 1993.

Cabrera, James C., and Albrecht, Charles F., Jr. *The Lifetime Career Manager: New Strategies for a New Era*. Holbrook, MA: Adams Publishing, 1995.

Carter, Carol; Lyman Kravits, Sarah; and Spencer Vaughan, Patricia. *The Career Tool Kit: Skills for Success*. Englewood Cliffs, NJ: Prentice-Hall, 1995.

Clawson, James G.; Kotter, John P.; Faux, Victor A.; and McArthur, Charles C. *Self-Assessment and Career Development*. Third Edition. Englewood Cliffs, NJ: Prentice-Hall, 1992.

Drake, John D., Ph.D. *The Campus Interview*. New York: Drake Beam Morin, Inc., 1981.

Fein, Richard. *First Job: A New Grad's Guide to Launching Your Business Career*. New York: John Wiley & Sons, Inc., 1992.

Fox, Marcia R. *Put Your Degree to Work: The New Professional's Guide to Career Planning and Job Hunting*. New York: W. W. Norton & Company, 1988.

Keirsey, David, and Bates, Marilyn. *Please Understand Me: Character & Temperament Types*, Prometheus Nemesis Book Company, Del Mar, CA, 1984.

Kroeger, Otto, and Thuesen, Janet M. *Type Talk at Work*, Dell Publishing, New York, NY, 1992.

Managing Stress in Turbulent Times. New York: DBM Publishing, 1993.

Morin, William J., and Cabrera, James C. *Parting Company: How to Survive the Loss of a Job and Find Another Successfully*. San Diego, CA: Harcourt Brace Jovanovich, 1991.

Pedersen, Laura. *Street-Smart Career Guide: A Step-By-Step Program for Your Career Development*. New York: Crown Publishers, Inc., 1993.

Ritti, R. Richard. *The Ropes to Skip and the Ropes to Know: Studies in Organizational Behavior*. Fourth Edition. New York: John Wiley & Sons, 1994.

Rogers, Edward J. *Getting Hired: Everything You Need to Know about Resumes, Interviews, and Job-Hunting Strategies*. New York: Prentice-Hall, 1982.

Scheetz, L. Patrick. *Recruiting Trends 1994–1995*. East Lansing, MI: Collegiate Employment Research Institute, Michigan State University, 1994.

Schmidt, Peggy. *Making It On Your First Job*. Revised Edition. Princeton, NJ: Peterson's Guides, 1991.

Seven Imperatives for Fair, Legal and Productive Interviewing. New York: DBM Publishing, 1993.

Strasser, Stephen, and Sena, John. *From Campus to Corporation*. Hawthorne, NJ: Career Press, 1993.

Tieger, Paul D., and Barron-Tieger, Barbara. *Do What You Are*. Boston, MA: Little, Brown and Company, 1992.

Yeager, Neil. *Career Map*. New York, NY: John Wiley & Sons, Inc., 1988.

Yena, Donna J. *Career Directions*. Second Edition. Burr Ridge, IL: Irwin, 1993.

Index

Acknowledgments

Many people played an important role in bringing this project to fruition and giving it life. There are a number of people whom the author, publisher, and editors wish to thank personally for their words of wisdom—Phil Decker, Kevin Harrington, Dick Hess, John Kniering, Ed Ryan, Patrick Scheetz, and Laura Volz. Also, Sue Carta, who showed a lot of patience during the development and proofreading stages. And a special thanks to RB, without whose words this would not have been possible.

About the Editors

PAT MORTON is Senior Vice President at Drake Beam Morin, Inc. She has served in senior management positions in human resources for more than 15 years with HBO (health care information systems) in Atlanta and Motorola in Dallas, Connecticut, and California. Pat currently serves on the faculty of New York University, teaching courses in Human Resources and Training Measurement and Starting a Career in Human Resources.

MARCIA R. FOX, PH.D. is Group Vice President, Development at Drake Beam Morin, Inc. in New York, Prior to joining Drake Beam Morin in 1986, Marcia was an internal consultant and training specialist at Mobil Oil Corporation. Previously, she was Assistant Dean at New York University School of Public Administration, where she was in charge of career counseling and placement services. A professional writer in the career development field, she is the author of *Put Your Degree to Work,* a career planning and job-hunting guide for new professionals (W.W. Norton). Her articles on job search skills have appeared in *The New York Times, Mademoiselle,* and other publications.